GANG LIFE

PRAISE FOR *GANG LIFE*

"Anyone who thinks Canada does not have a serious gang-violence problem should take off their rose-coloured glasses and read Mark Totten's chilling book."

— Robert Rotenberg, author of *Stranglehold*

"Messy, sometimes tender, always brutal, Mark Totten's stories of ten different gang-bangers all inhabit the feral streets of our inner cities. In clear and unsentimental prose he draws a line from early poverty and abuse towards addiction and violence, a line as straight and undeniable as destiny."

—Stephen Reid, author of *A Crowbar in the Buddhist Garden*

"Hidden under the cloak of anonymity these ten criminals are able to tell their tales of their lost worlds with brutal honesty. A triumph in exploring the depths of the drug addicted and how their unrelenting struggle keeps them in a life of crime. While at times it felt as though I was reading a biographical news article, I applaud Mark Totten for being able to bring these people's stories to life in their own words."

—Ranj Dhaliwal, author of *Daaku: The Gangster's Life*

"Mark Totten has done a masterful job humanizing the lives of gangsters. The stories told on the pages of this book make it impossible not to appreciate how our social environment has influenced the choices of gang members. However we choose to define the nebulous concept of gangs, Totten's participants ardently embraced and lived a lifestyle that few of us can comprehend. They adopted behaviours and a set of values that spawn fear and loathing within the mainstream social order. The time, effort, and risk that Mark assumed in gaining the trust of these individuals so their stories can be told is praiseworthy and priceless. The openness with which these gang members shared their lives is equally courageous and commendable. Their stories illustrate in very real ways that, while accountability plays an important role, penance alone can never eliminate the reality of this thriving underground culture. Gangs and gangsters will continue to devastate lives until society understands and accepts its role in compassionately and proactively addressing the challenges that drive our youth to such a destructive way of life."

— Superintendent, Bob Mills, RCMP, Regina, SK

"Dr. Totten's brave new book, *Gang Life*, provides an extremely rare and remarkably insightful examination of the violent, troubled, and often shortened lives of individual gang members. Often gleaned at personal peril, the qualitative research on which this book is based represents an extraordinary accomplishment. I feel this book should be recommended reading for all academics and front line workers in addition to all those who seek a better understanding gang life. Through a honest and realistic understanding of these individuals we can begin to make meaningful change."

— Peggy Rubin, Executive Director,
Prince Albert Outreach Program Inc.

"Although there is no shortage of books written by 'experts' on gangs, this book offers a visceral accounting about the lives of ten (former) high profile Canadian gang members. Capitalizing on his twenty-five years of related work with gangs and gang members, Totten offers a refreshing yet provocative insight not only about the 'how' of gang life but more importantly the 'why' of gang involvement. Totten's unbiased accounting of their stories, although perhaps controversial, does not glorify gang life but draws clear and objective attention to the need for a paradigm shift if we are ever going to effectively address the gang problem in society. Few studies, let alone books, offer the level of insight that is presented in this book. A must read for anyone interested in human and social welfare."

— John Winterdyk, Professor of Justice Studies,
Mount Royal University

"*Gang Life* is a well written book that depicts the lives of ten ex-gang members. The stories portray the truthful and honest experience endured by [ex-gang members] as children. As many are of aboriginal descent, I am aware that storytelling is a big part of the healing process in giving a voice. Reading their stories not only makes one feel compassion, but motivation to help children in the system that binds them and that could potentially bring more harm than good. The book instills hope in all the work that we do and would be an excellent resource for foster parents, social workers, teachers and many other professionals who work with youth at risk."

— Stella Bone, Executive Director,
West Region Child and Family Services, Winnipeg

"*Gang Life* helps us to understand why young people join gangs by capturing young people's own life stories. Detailed accounts of lives lived in dangerous and chaotic environments are provided without the usual editorializing. Instead, Mark Totten gently organizes these stories of heartbreaking pasts, violence, and addictions into clear but gritty narratives. The end result is a unique book that shows us why violence and crime is a path that makes sense to some. Each story, while different, shares many of the same themes: loss, trauma, and a search for belonging and something powerful to say about one's self. For these individuals, all of them ex-gang members, gangs were a solution to problems that they couldn't solve in other ways. This is a powerful inside look at lives about which we hear a great deal but seldom take the time to really understand. Totten does a wonderful job of giving them voice, making these individuals seem much more human, and more vulnerable, than we might want to believe."

— Michael Ungar, Network Director, Children and Youth in Challenging Contexts (CYCC) Network and Co-Director, Resilience Research Centre Dalhousie University

"Gangs are not just a police problem, they are a community problem. These kids hit a fork in the road and decide to join a gang. *Gang Life* looks at a desensitized generation that does not understand the deadly consequences of the abuse, manipulation and violence that define gangs. Totten's book looks at the gaps and pressures we have in our social agencies, and addresses how we can stop our youth from choosing to live a gang life. Social justice issues need to be kept at the forefront, and Totten's work is a valuable contribution to that discussion."

— Dave Shuttleworth, Inspector, Contract and Aboriginal Policing, RCMP D Division, Winnipeg, Manitoba

ALSO BY MARK TOTTEN:

Nasty, Brutish and Short:
The Lives of Gang Members in Canada

GANG LIFE

10 of the Toughest Tell Their Stories

MARK TOTTEN
WITH THE ASSISTANCE OF KAILA TOTTEN

JAMES LORIMER & COMPANY LTD., PUBLISHERS
TORONTO

James Lorimer & Company Ltd., Publishers acknowledges the support of the Ontario Arts Council. We acknowledge the financial support of the Government of Canada through the Canada Book Fund for our publishing activities. We acknowledge the support of the Canada Council for the Arts which last year invested $24.3 million in writing and publishing throughout Canada. We acknowledge the Government of Ontario through the Ontario Media Development Corporation's Ontario Book Initiative.

Cover image: iStock
Cover design: Meredith Bangay

Library and Archives Canada Cataloguing in Publication

Totten, Mark Douglas, 1962-, author
    Gang life : 10 of the toughest tell their stories / Mark Totten.

Issued in print and electronic formats.
ISBN 978-1-4594-0625-4 (pbk.).--ISBN 978-1-4594-0627-8 (epub)

    1. Gangs--Canada. 2. Gang members--Canada. I. Title.

HV6439.C3T65 2014   364.106'60971   C2013-907871-1
C2013-907872-X

James Lorimer & Company Ltd., Publishers
317 Adelaide Street West, Suite 1002
Toronto, ON, Canada
M5V 1P9
www.lorimer.ca

Printed and bound in Canada.

*For Rita Dunn and Alice Carolyn McLurg,
two of the most amazing and compassionate
women you will ever meet.
I owe much of who I am to you both.*

TABLE OF CONTENTS

✷ INTRODUCTION ✷

This book tells the true stories of some of the most violent people in Canada who are involved in some of the most notorious gangs this country has ever seen. You will not find much analysis in *Gang Life — Ten of the Toughest Tell Their Stories*, because that's not the kind of book it is. The words of the ten gang members included here do the talking.

It is up to you to make up your mind about what these people are saying. The stories they tell may shock you, even make you look at your country in a different light. Ordinary law-abiding Canadians will not find here the Canada they know, where we like to think most people feel relatively safe and protected. In contrast, students and professors of social work and criminology may find a more familiar landscape. I hope they will also find much here that is new to them, and that it can illuminate and illustrate their work.

I became interested in gangs about twenty-five years ago when I was volunteering for the John Howard Society in Kingston Penitentiary. I had also worked for a couple of years in social housing projects in Ottawa, where gang activity was percolating but by no means common. In 1992 I began my doctoral studies in Sociology at Carleton University and focused my work on youth violence and gangs. I found out quickly that I really had no idea how little I knew about this field.

So, what exactly do I mean by "gang"? In my experience I've heard the word used to cover anything from a number of kids playing together in a park to organized groups of criminals with a clear hierarchy and rules that govern the group's behaviour. I prefer to use a tight definition, including three major types of gangs: street gangs, mid-level gangs, and organized crime groups. All three types have relationships with other gangs that are fluid and opportunistic, often organized around lucrative criminal opportunities. All three are involved in serious and violent crimes, although organized crime groups tend to fly under the radar of the police, whereas the two other types of gangs are more brazen and less sophisticated. Family bloodlines are important for all three types.

Street gangs are visible, hardcore groups that come together for profit-driven criminal activity; they are often brutally violent. Gang-related communication rituals, such as complicated handshakes, and public display of gang-like attributes, such as tattoos, are common. Street gangs have some stability over time, yet membership is fluid. They typically claim an area or turf, which they protect from rival gangs. This may be a housing project or an area they claim to be their own for drug distribution. You may have noticed kids hanging around together, sporting the same clothes in the same colours: pants belted low, hooded sweatshirts, bandanas, and ball caps. Perhaps you've noticed running shoes tied together and slung high over a telephone wire or the same graffiti sprayed on bare walls throughout certain neighbourhoods of your city. Did you realize that what you're seeing are the identification markers for a street gang? Like mid-level gangs, street gangs rely on violent entry and exit rituals — vicious beatings for men, beatings or gang rapes for women — to protect them from outsiders. Marginalized ethnic and racial minorities, including Aboriginal peoples, dominate membership. While some gangs have members mainly from a single ethnic group, an increasing number have a multi-ethnic membership. One key factor that differentiates many of those who become involved in street gangs from those who don't is the experience of acute poverty.

Mid-level gangs have characteristics of both street gangs and organized crime groups. They can be multi-ethnic, although some groups in the prairie provinces are exclusively Aboriginal. Members may come from different socio-economic backgrounds, but Aboriginal and black gang members have lived in extreme poverty. These gangs frequently form in schools, young offender centres, and foster homes. Compared to organized crime groups, mid-level gangs are made up of unstructured smaller groups or cells, although they are frequently sophisticated and disciplined.

Organized crime groups are highly structured and hierarchical; in this, they model successful companies with their entrenched rules, by-laws, and constitutions. They have flourished over time and are recognized, feared, and respected. Their exclusive memberships are based on family, race, and ethnicity.

In 2007, I began evaluating a couple of multi-year gang intervention and prevention projects in Canada. I also had the good fortune to work with other groups across the country, including police forces and municipalities, to develop anti-gang strategies and programs for gang members who wanted to leave the life. In addition, I started work with a couple of semi-remote Aboriginal communities. The focus of those latter projects is to interrupt cycles of violence on reserves. This includes addressing domestic violence, dating violence, sexual abuse and commercial sexual exploitation, bullying, lateral violence, gang violence, and anything else that falls in-between these labels.

Along the way, I have met, counselled, interviewed, and researched hundreds of gang members: young and old; male, female, transgender, gay, lesbian, and bisexual; Aboriginal, black, Asian, Latino, Caucasian, and multi-ethnic; presidents, soldiers, treasurers, debt collectors, runners, new recruits, and wannabes; those in prisons and those on the street; organized crime groups (such as the Hells Angels, MS-13, and the Russian Mafia), mid-level gangs (such as Native Syndicate and United Nations), and disorganized street gangs (such as the African Mafia, Malvern Crew, and the Ledbury-Banff Crips).

I want to understand gang members' use of violence and involvement in crime from their perspective and trace their lives from infancy to adulthood. I've had the good fortune to work in jobs where I have spent lots of time getting to know gang members and building trust with them. Through the many qualitative and quantitative studies I've conducted over the years, I've spent a lot of time hanging out with gangs, getting to know the members, and building trust. When I feel they are comfortable with my role, and with me, I ask them if they would consent to participate in confidential, audiotaped, in-depth interviews. I've used several interview methods to gather information such as structured questionnaires or asking open-ended questions, such as "Tell me about your involvement in gangs," "What was growing up like?" and "Have you ever thought of leaving?" Although some gang members think I'm a bit odd for my interest in their lives, they are often very forthcoming in telling their stories in their own words.

I admit I've been scared a few times. Once, Sharon (my partner) and I took a group of youth on a camping expedition to a lake in eastern Ontario. Late that night, we were jolted awake by the sound of gunshots fired in our direction. I waded into the water with a flashlight to find out what was going on. A man in a motorboat took off when he saw me coming. Later, we found out that he had serious mental health problems, had just been released from a hospital, and was drunk. He'd gone out in his boat to shoot at lights along the shore. Our campfire made an easy target.

Then, when I was working as a protection social worker with the Children's Aid Society, I had an unnerving experience. I had taken a toddler into hospital for medical attention and photographing of his many bruises. He had been severely beaten. The parents were agitated, sensing that I was going to apprehend their child. When I told them that the child would be going to a foster home, the father lunged over a table and tried to choke me, in the presence of four police officers. One restraining order and a couple of charges later, the father left me alone. It was uncomfortable testifying against him in court, but he was convicted of uttering threats and assault.

Most recently, during one of the interviews for this book, a gang member high on crack took a couple of swings at me. I dove off the deck of his house and ended up headfirst in a snowbank.

Although I was fearful in these situations, I have to say that these incidents were rare. Perhaps the reader will find this surprising. My belief is that if you treat people with respect and are honest, you will get the same in return, no matter how violent people might be. You also have to be smart and not put yourself in situations where you could get harmed. And perhaps fear is a motivator for my writing — not really my own fear, but that of the general public with regards to gang members. Yes, my participants have done pretty horrendous things, but they are people after all — parents, sons, daughters, brothers, and sisters. They were not born bad, but instead came to do bad things as a result of their personal and social experiences.

One thing this book must do is protect the anonymity of my informants because they all have been involved in high-profile gangs and have committed easily recognizable crimes. Ensuring their safety is a key condition of allowing me to interview them. Without this, they could be severely assaulted, or even killed, by other gang members. They could also face serious challenges finding work or in other areas of their lives, despite having left the gang life years ago.

In addition to maintaining confidentiality, I have to make it clear that I have legal and moral obligations to inform the relevant authorities if I find out the people I'm interviewing are involved in any serious crimes or have done serious harm to others. The key issue here is what constitutes "serious" crime and "serious" harm — I mean cases where the police are not aware of murder or assaults so savage that the victim may die. Child welfare officials have to be informed if I discover that children are being abused. Mental health professionals have to be contacted if gang members are suicidal or have indicators of serious mental illness. The police have to be informed if there is life-threatening harm. I did not have to report any of the participants in *Gang Life: Ten of the Toughest Tell Their Stories* to the authorities because their actions were no surprise to the police, child welfare, or mental health sectors — all systems were on top of these situations.

With the permission of the ten participants, I have reproduced their narratives — their spoken words — and woven them into what I believe are coherent stories. For some, this is difficult because their narratives are chaotic and disjointed. For others, it is much easier because of their higher level of literacy and more logical thinking patterns. Each participant has a fictitious name. Because many of the participants have been involved in high-profile gang crimes, I have altered their stories in minor ways to protect them.

I know the participants very well, and they, likewise, know me. Some I met ten or more years ago as a social worker and researcher, others I got to know more recently when looking for people to interview for this book. I meet lots of gang members in the context of my work, but very few are open to telling their life stories. You can't just sit down and record conversations with people you don't know, let alone hardened gangsters. It takes considerable time to build trust and establish a level of comfort. I spent many months getting to know my informants prior to turning my recorder on. They, in turn, put considerable thought into whether, and under what conditions, they might want to open up their lives to me.

So, who are these participants? All ten, including three women, say they are ex-gang members, who have been out of gang life anywhere between one and five years, though they still have good friends who are involved in their old gangs and keep them up to speed on gang activities. Their ages range from twenty-five to forty-one years. Three of the men immigrated to Canada at a young age with their families to flee civil wars — one from Sudan, one from a South American country, and another from an Eastern European country. Of the remaining seven who were born in Canada, two are Cree, two are Métis, two are Caucasian, and one is mixed race from black and Caucasian parents. They come from all across the country: two grew up and are living in British Columbia, two are in Alberta, three in Saskatchewan, one in Manitoba, one in Ontario, and one was raised and is living in the Maritimes. And they live in all kinds of communities: two are currently living on semi-remote small reserves with a population of 500 band members or less, two are in cities with a population less than 30,000, three are living in medium-sized cities with a population of roughly 300,000, and three are living in large cities with a population of over one million.

It is interesting that most of the participants indicated that it is perfectly natural for ethnic and racial groups to align against one another in their neighbourhoods as well in the gangs. Some spoke openly about their hatred for certain minority groups.

All of them are users and, most of them, abusers of drugs and alcohol. Only one person was never addicted, although she drinks and smokes weed regularly. Three are still hard-core addicts who, for many years, have abused crack, alcohol, prescription narcotics, crystal methamphetamine, and anything else they can get their hands on. These three are also still involved in low-level drug dealing and other crimes, including assaults, break and enters, and fencing stolen goods. Two injected morphine and cocaine for a long time; both are clean, but one drinks. Two more have overcome addictions to cocaine and alcohol, although both still drink regularly. The remaining two have stopped abusing alcohol and marijuana; one is clean and the other drinks occasionally. Three of the men, who regularly injected steroids throughout their gang involvement, were heavily involved in the trafficking of steroids and human growth hormones.

The participants played a variety of roles in their gangs. Of the seven men, two were enforcers and debt collectors (each played both roles); two ran a drug crew in their gang; one was a drug, gun, and money transporter; and two were presidents (leaders) of their respective gangs. Of the three women, two founded their own gangs and were leaders, and the third was a soldier who ran a sophisticated cocaine and prostitution network.

The participants also represent the three types of gangs discussed above: six were involved in highly organized mid-level gangs, three were involved in chaotic street gangs, and one ran the Canadian chapter of a multinational organized crime group. Three of the mid-level gang members were associates of Canadian chapters of international outlaw motorcycle gangs. Their own gangs and the biker gangs worked in close partnership in the trafficking of drugs, guns, and women. They also played enforcement and debt collector roles for these biker gangs.

All of them witnessed, participated in, and/or have been victims of savage violence. They witnessed murders or were directly involved in killing someone. Eight took part in torturing people who owed the gang money or who had ripped off a fellow gang member. The remaining two said that they had been present when such attacks took place but did not participate in them. Not only did they inflict violence on other people, but they also harmed themselves: five had attempted suicide multiple times, and the remaining five had taken part in self-destructive behaviours for most of their lives, such as cutting, burning, and punching brick walls with their bare fists or heads.

Nine of the participants reflected the common trait of traumatic childhoods filled with abuse, abandonment, rejection, and parental addictions. Three were adopted and five bounced around in many foster homes, constantly running away and then being sent back to the same or different homes. Six had been sexually abused when they were kids, many times by caregivers (adult family members or foster fathers). The one young man who says his parents are good had serious emotional and behavioural disorders as a child, which his parents were unable to address.

In spite of this similar heritage of childhood trauma, their socio-economic backgrounds vary. Four grew up in affluent families, in homes they call a "nice place"; they never went without during their childhood and, even now, their lives remain comfortable. The remaining six have always lived in abject poverty and continue to struggle to meet their basic needs. Three are on social assistance and live in social housing, and another works for minimum wage and lives in subsidized housing. The other two live on the street and are often homeless. Despite the harsh realities of their stories, I want to remain true to the narratives of my informants. I believe that this gives the reader a keen sense of the uniqueness of their lives.

In spite of their own difficult lives, eight of the participants have children, either by accident or on purpose. Only four of them have custody of their children. The four who do not are addicts, live in violence, and are unstably housed. Of those who have children, all but two have multiple children.

Most of the participants have tried hard to create a life after the gang that will allow them to bring their children up in a better world than they experienced. None of them want their children involved in gangs, although they often don't have complete control over their adolescent children's choices. Three participants have completed college or university degrees and a fourth is partway through a university degree. Three others completed high school as mature students, but the remaining three, who dropped out of elementary school, still have a low level of literacy. Half of them hold jobs: one is a heavy machine mechanic, another is an engineer, one is a manager of a clothing store, one works in the social services, and one works part-time as a manual labourer. The others are on social assistance or are living on the street.

In Chapter One, twenty-five-year-old Kim describes a life, both inside and outside her gang, in which "I did not know who I was." Her childhood and early adolescence were wracked with rejection and abandonment, and she bounced around from family to foster homes for many years. She left her gang when she was nineteen. A Cree, she had no attachment to her culture. She started to develop an identity a couple of years ago, following the birth of her son and after getting to know some Cree Elders.

Chapter Two tells the story of thirty-three-year-old Terrence, a mixed race "independent enforcer" who found the Lord just in time for a parole hearing. Terrence has a rather large ego and he leaves us with the impression that he thinks he may be Jesus. Terrence lets us in on the world of gang "contractors" — those who refuse to join gangs but contract out their services to many different gangs. Often in steroid-fuelled rages, his violence is extreme — both against others and himself. As a youngster, professionals gave up on him, but his parents never stopped trying to get him help. He has a young son and is struggling to overcome his addiction to crack.

We are introduced in Chapter Three to Monica, a forty-five-year-old lesbian gang mother. Now clean after too many years of injecting morphine and cocaine, she takes in young gang members and cares for them. She was terrorized by a foster father and attributes her sexual orientation to his sexual violence. She founded her gang over twenty years ago and ran a gang house for decades. Monica has a chaotic notion of "mothering." She tries her best to parent her own four children and over one dozen grandchildren even though most are in foster care. Yet, almost all of the young gang members she welcomes into her home are on the run from foster and group homes.

In Chapter Four, Jake, who is Caucasian and twenty-eight years old, takes us on a whirlwind tour that parallels the emotional and behavioural problems that plagued his childhood with his life in a gang. He was adopted as a toddler into an affluent home with good parents. A slave to his emotions and lack of impulse control, the allure of money, women, and drugs impelled him to join one of the fiercest gangs in Western Canada. He was an enforcer and debt collector not only for his own gang, but also for a biker gang. He came by his obsession with toughness honestly — his father modelled and rewarded Jake with this behaviour when he was a youngster. Jake never backed down from a confrontation and now, out of the gang for a couple of years, he is not backing down from the challenges of creating a new life for himself.

The story of Janie, aged twenty-five, and George, eight years older, is in Chapter Five. Both Aboriginal, they were married until George killed a rival a couple of years ago. He also tried to kill Janie, both when they were together and again when he was in prison for the murder. He put a hit out on her because he was not happy that she was divorcing him and was afraid of what secrets she might tell. George, who was vice-president for years before becoming president, courted Janie from the time she was thirteen until after she joined his gang. Her mother was involved with the same gang so Janie was seduced by the promise of easy money and a never-ending supply of morphine and crack. Janie became queen of her gang, an auxiliary to George's male-dominated gang. Good with money, she was the treasurer of his gang as well as her own. Janie has five children and believes that if she keeps busy as a parent, she will forget the sexual abuse she suffered during her childhood.

Dillon, aged thirty-three and a Latino father of two, tells his story in Chapter Six. Along with five friends, he founded a gang in high school. A few years later he was asked to patch over and lead the Canadian chapter of a large multinational gang. His gang was into drug and gun trafficking and inflicting violence on anyone in their way. Dillon now plays in a jazz band and regularly speaks to groups of young people about the dangers of gangs and drugs.

Gilbert, a Métis man aged thirty-four years, and Maureen, thirty-five years, live on a small reserve. Their lives are described in Chapter Seven. Both are hard-core addicts and have two boys who have been adopted. Their relationship is a powder keg and they spend just as much time fighting as they spend partying. When he associated with gangs, Gilbert ran his own drug crew and, like Terrence, contracted out his services to a biker gang, as well as to black and Aboriginal gangs. He is a hustler and has been on the street since his mother abandoned him as a young child. It's a good thing that he has been forbidden to possess weapons. His life is confined: when not locked up in jail, he fights in cages in mixed martial arts competitions.

In Chapter Eight, we meet thirty-two-year-old Jeremy and thirty-year-old Dawn. Jeremy is a scrawny transporter of guns, drugs, and money for various gangs. Despite having Aboriginal blood, he passes as white, which he uses to his advantage as much as he can. He is a hard-core alcoholic and crack user, as is his wife Dawn. He is fond of saying, "If I told you, I'd have to kill you," by which he means if he discloses too much about his involvement in serious gang crimes, he would have to take my life to prevent me from telling anyone else these details. He has served time for beating two men so viciously that they are now brain-damaged. His reason for assaulting them was that he believed they had harmed women, something he will not tolerate in others, but he routinely beats his wife. Dawn has AIDS but doesn't protect herself when working the streets, nor does Jeremy protect himself when they are having sex. Both are comfortable living on the streets, but they were living on a reserve at the time we met.

Jafar, a Sudanese refugee and father of two, recounts a harrowing story in Chapter Nine. When he was four years old, his family fled a civil war that had taken the lives of many relatives. He witnessed atrocities and endured a four-month trek to Egypt on foot, by boat, and by train. His parents were looking for a better life but did not find it in Canada. Jafar led a vicious street gang that had splintered from a larger gang over a dispute. He brought rules and order to what was then a disorganized group of thugs from Sub-Saharan Africa, but he grew disillusioned a couple of years later. From jail, he witnessed his gang spiral into confusion in the leadership vacuum. Jafar has turned his life around following his exit from gang life. Now twenty-nine years old and facing deportation for his crimes, he has been out of gang life for four years. He is clean and sober, has completed high school and college, and works full time with a social agency.

The story of Ivan is told in Chapter Ten. He is forty-one years of age, and he came to Canada as a young boy when his family — mother, stepfather, and younger brother — fled a civil war in their Eastern European country. The family was plagued by alcoholism and his stepfather instilled in Ivan the code of the street: don't rat, don't trust the police, and fight for your family honour. To this day Ivan bears the heavy burden of supporting his mentally ill mother and his siblings. Ivan played a specialized role in his high-profile gang — he was responsible for negotiating the "terms and conditions" of cocaine and gun trafficking with a South American cartel. Ivan was a higher-up and led his own crew. They not only trafficked in illicit drugs, but they also imported steroids and human growth hormones from other countries. He believed in showing the value of his product to potential customers: no one in his crew weighed less than 240 pounds of solid muscle.

With the exception of one individual, these are gang members who have never been portrayed in any of my earlier publications. Some I have known for a couple of years, others I met just before their interviews for this book. Those who have read *Nasty, Brutish and Short* may recognize bits and pieces of one person's story, but I have presented only new narratives in *Gang Life: Ten of the Toughest Tell Their Stories*.

I make no apologies for the raw, violent, and explicit nature of the language in their narratives. Their voices are real. They have bared their lives for readers and in return I need to honour their lives.

✳ CHAPTER 1 ✳

I DID NOT KNOW WHO
I WAS

Kim, a beautiful Cree woman, is twenty-five years old, solid and strong. She reminds me of a slimmer, feminine version of a sumo wrestler — without the chonmage *(samurai pony tail) and loincloth. Every day she proudly sports a different set of fingernails. She spends hours prying off old nails and gluing on new ones. She likes long nails in dark colours — black, purple, red — or designs: beads, animals, and faces. She is also obsessed with eyebrows. Hers are usually black arches, highlighted with a touch of blue. She has the perfect solution to incorrigible, bushy ones: "Pull 'em out and paint the fuckers on."*

She is also fond of piercings and tattoos. She has a small diamond earring in the centre of her nose and another piercing in her tongue. She is fond of rattling the silver bead on her tongue against her teeth, especially when she wants to annoy the hell out of police or her parole officer. She has many tattoos, most of them related to her gang. I can't describe them because that would reveal not only the name of her gang, but perhaps her identity.

At just under six feet, she is an imposing figure. Her hair, halfway down her back and jet black, is always perfectly coiffed. Her mascara-coated eyelashes match her figure: wide, long, and striking. Once I asked her how she put that goop on her eyelids without going blind. She laughed and told me that she would do mine next. Most days she also has on blue eyeliner. This gives her a mystical air. My first impression is that she is a warrior princess, and a very loud one at that. It's hard to see her as the hard-core gang member she once was.

I met Kim in November 2007, in a mid-size city in the prairies. Neither Kim nor I were dressed for the weather that day, and we both shivered uncontrollably even as we shook hands. It was cold as hell outside, at least minus forty degrees Celsius, and just as cold inside. The building was in sad shape. The pipes had burst and a small river was flowing through the room next to us. All the doors were open and city workers in waist-high gaiters were traipsing in and out. A water main on the street had also burst; the street and parking lot had become one large skating rink. Giant icicles hung off hydro wires and trees, and the air was dense with crystallized ice. The city workers were shouting and some hidden machine made a tremendous racket.

The building was situated in a neighbourhood where seven gangs were active. The city is chronically identified as one of the most dangerous places in the country, and this particular neighbourhood ranks as one of the worst in Canada. The population is highly transient; poverty and homelessness are common, as is the street sex trade. Drug dealing takes place on every street corner and kids can be seen wandering the streets not only late at night, but also during the day. They aren't in school because they have been kicked out, dropped out, or are taking a holiday from classes. They come from families where caregivers have low levels of literacy and don't see school as a way out of poverty and hopelessness.

The building housed an anti-gang project, which is how I met Kim. The building itself had a brick exterior and few windows. A security system with cameras had been installed but was not working. This made me a bit uneasy because anyone could wander through the door. The staff members were not in the habit of checking whom they let in. They merely pushed a button in the main office when someone rang the bell, even though gang leaders were known to "troll" gang programs for their own underlings who might be thinking of leaving or spilling the beans on what the gang was up to.

Needless to say, my first encounter with Kim did not last long. Our teeth chattered as we talked, mostly about the deplorable conditions inside and outside the office. I asked Kim a couple of questions about her family and she talked full-speed for some time. She indicated that she was no longer in her gang, but I got the sense that this really depended on whomever she was hanging with on any given day. People like Kim can exit a gang officially, yet still maintain ties for years with friends and family who are gang-involved.

I met Kim about a dozen times each year over the project's five-year tenure. She gave me the minutest of details about her life: where she came from; her childhood, adolescence, adulthood, family, and boyfriends; her gang involvement and exit; and her involvement in crime. She told me about her deepest secrets and her hopes for the future. Like a roller coaster, she was up, down, and all around, taking two steps forward, and more often than not, two back, then three ahead. She careened from one experience to another: school, jobs, partying, the street. But she still managed to inch forward. Her intimate relationships were somewhat chaotic and she bounced from man to man. But, throughout this time, she maintained her sense of humour and boisterous laugh.

That laugh let me know when Kim was around. She is so

loud and fond of expletives. She believes she invented the word "fuck" and any related adjective, verb, and noun: "Fuck you, you motherfucker, that's fucking awesome." She blows into the room like a tsunami and fills it to bursting. She means business and will tell you if you are full of shit. I consider myself quite lucky that I experienced her anger only a couple times. Once, she exploded into the office, yelling profanities at everyone. We were all too scared not to pay attention. She was mad at a staff member who she believed had made sexual advances to her best friend, Tina. Like the king-size Slurpee she often carries, she is oversized and prone to freezing your brain if you step out of line. There is a part of Kim that enjoys the fear she can instill in you. She manages to hide it well until it bursts out occasionally in response to situations where she feels threatened.

Kim's stone-cold reputation on the street seemed out of sync with her care for her feminine appearance. She referred to herself as "one tough-ass bitch": cross her and you better run. She was much tougher than her nails and eyebrows suggested and left many victims in her wake of rage and violence. This is what struck me most about Kim: behind her feminine mask she had a brutal, masculine side. She navigated her gender around landmines. A survivor, she could use her sexuality to disarm men, yet she could draw on toughness and violence to instill fear in those who posed a threat to her or those close to her.

Kim dropped her rag (left her gang) in March 2008 at the age of nineteen. She had been a "higher-up" in a well-established Aboriginal street gang from the time she was fourteen; she was the only woman among the gang leadership. Five young men, all acquaintances of Kim, formed the gang in the early 1990s, although she did not know them well until she was down with them (associated with them) for a couple months. Despite its chaotic nature on the streets, where the leadership control over members was fractured by rivalry, the gang was interprovincial and had highly organized cells in many provinces across the country.

Kim had lived a difficult life prior to joining. Her biological father and mother were both hard-core addicts, injecting morphine and other drugs. Her mother worked in the sex trade for most of her life, and her father had dealt drugs and pimped out young women for many years.

Kim's grandmother, Noni, took her at birth but did not adopt her. Noni is a fanatical Saskatchewan Roughriders fan. More often than not she wears a T-shirt sporting the team's logo, a shirt she seldom washes. When I met her, she was seventy years of age and wore a pair of glasses, the kind with small oval lenses, perched on her rather large, red nose. Almost as tall as her granddaughter, she has high cheekbones and a generous chin. When she smiles, her head cocks to one side. Her thin and wispy hair is often tied up in a bun. Like Kim, she is tougher than nails.

Noni sports the tell-tale signs of an alcoholic: her face is always beet red and flushed, the skin on her arms is yellowed, likely the result of cirrhosis. The teeth she still has are decayed, brown. Her hands tremor as soon as she gets out of bed; the tremors stop only after her first drink. She has chronic diarrhea and usually makes a couple of mad dashes to the toilet every day. She suffers constant lung infections and has contracted pneumonia too many times to count.

Kim met her biological mother when she was six. Noni, who was drinking heavily at the time, had sent her to live with her biological mother for one month while she went on vacation to Niagara Falls with her drug-dealing boyfriend. Kim said her mother was "staying with a trick, she was with an older man. [I] could not believe that she was with an older man. What was she doing? He was her mark [sugar daddy]." Kim had no idea who this woman was and remembered being sent out to play in a ghetto among drug addicts and alcoholics.

One day, Kim stepped on a sewing needle on the floor. While her mother was taking it out of her foot, she instructed Kim to tell Noni that the needle was not for injecting drugs but was just a sewing needle. She told Kim this over and over again. Kim was too young to understand that her biological mother was an intravenous drug abuser and that she was not allowed to care for her. "I looked at her and I just didn't know why she said that. I was just a little girl. I thought, like, 'Why do I need to say that? Wouldn't she already know?' That was before I knew about the drugs and shit. But then it clicked in."

Noni raised Kim until about age eight, at which time she was apprehended and placed in a foster home. Noni was a good person and desperately wanted to care for her granddaughter, but, like Kim's biological mother, she was an addict. Her boyfriends were also addicts and drug dealers and ran women on the streets. Kim endured physical abuse when Noni was drinking: "It was nothin' I could not handle. I had to be tough since I was a little girl. But it made me feel like it was a mistake for her to take me in."

To this day Kim remembers the exact circumstances that led to her being taken away from her grandmother the first time. She had brought a friend home after school. Noni's current boyfriend was doing needles at the kitchen table with five or six sex trade workers. The friend went home and told her mother what was going on at Kim's place. The mother called social services, and a social worker came to interview Kim, Noni, and the boyfriend. The next day, Kim came home for lunch and found her grandmother weeping on the couch. Noni told Kim that she had to go with a social worker to a foster home. Kim asked why, but Noni shrugged her shoulders and told her she didn't know.

Kim lasted at this first place for about a month. School was difficult for Kim. She was placed in a new school that had only one other Aboriginal student. Everyone at the school assumed that because she was Aboriginal and did not start her school year in September, she was in the foster care system. "It kind of made me feel embarrassed. I knew that they were thinking: 'What's wrong with your family, and why are you in there?'" Quickly, she came to the conclusion that the only way to cope was to run.

Noni had to go into addictions treatment as a condition of getting Kim back. She was away for many months, but she was not able to stay off the alcohol and drugs when she came home. Kim returned home for a bit, and Noni took part in required counselling. But Kim was taken away again.

She ran away and was brought to a different home by her social worker. She ran away again and was again found a week or so later, when she was brought by the same social worker to a third foster home. She ran away again, and the cycle continued for another year or so.

The child welfare system finally gave up on her and left her bouncing around on the streets from age ten until age fourteen. These experiences contributed to a deep sense of rejection. Although she hated the foster homes and was already reeling from her grandmother's rejection, the fact that social workers gave up on her was like putting salt in her gaping wound. "I felt like social services just stopped looking for me. Like they just stopped trying to bring me back. Because after a while they just stopped chasing me, it was weird." By her own estimation, she had been in over twenty different group homes and foster homes across Saskatchewan and Manitoba over a two-year period. She usually ran back home to her grandmother.

To this very day, Kim still does not know why her grandmother put her in foster care and has not felt comfortable asking Noni why. "I don't know why she did that, I just don't. She didn't want to look after me. Why did she do that?" According to Kim, this initial experience of being rejected has turned into a lifelong struggle to figure out her identity. "I did not know who I was. I was lost." She was full of questions: Why was I taken away? Why can't my parents take care of me? Why am I one of only two Indian kids at school?

On top of this, she served many custodial sentences in young offender facilities. As a young offender, Kim racked up many convictions and was sentenced in total to five or six years in secure facilities and another couple of years on probation. At age twelve, she was convicted of auto theft. Kim told me that in her late teens, she was put on house arrest as a consequence of ongoing criminal involvement.

Kim discovered who her biological father was when she was twelve or thirteen. She had just been released from a young offender facility. "It was right after I got out. I met him after this. He had kids with other women. I had no real connection with anyone. He did not want kids but had no fucking problem making them." Her father was a heavy-duty drug dealer and always had sex trade workers in his place. They did needles together. Kim didn't understand what was going on. Why were all these women partying with her dad? Why were they sticking needles in their arms?

"My life was kinda shitty. I got nothing I am proud of growing up. It sucked."

Kim's brother, Andrew, eleven months older, had a very different experience. He grew up on reserve after having been taken at birth by their father's mother. "He had a better life. He had a better life than anybody. He is the only one out of all of us that doesn't have a criminal record, and he is just totally fuckin' different from me or anybody else. Like, if you ever met him you would be able to tell that he was in a different upbringing, I guess."

Kim didn't know her siblings well and they had never been close. This separation from her sister and brothers, which began when Kim was a young child, scarred Kim: "If my grandma would have took all of us, it would have been a lot different."

Kim's introduction to her gang was very unusual. She never hooked up with a male gang member, never worked the street, and never touched hard drugs. She was first exposed to gang life through partying with older males, some of whom were a part of the gang lifestyle. Kenny was one of her friends. His girlfriend was the first gang girl who experienced Kim's rage and violence. "I got into a fight with this lady. This chick kicked me in the face and I broke her nose. She was in her twenties and I was scared that I couldn't beat on her because she was much older.

"Then Kenny asked me if I wanted to be down [join the gang]. He texted me for a whole month and I said no, no, no. I was not forced but he kept on asking me and asking me. The gang wanted me in because I beat up this chick and I was so much younger. Everyone was all scared. What they didn't know was that I was scared too." Although she was not forced to join the gang, and she alone decided to become a member, she was pressured and pestered repeatedly by Kenny. This went on for quite some time. Finally, while drunk one night, she told him that she wanted to be down.

Many gang members that I spoke with believed Kenny to be one bad dude. He was a founding member of the gang and was moving up the hierarchy while Kim was still in diapers.

At five feet ten inches, he is built like a truck. He has a barrel chest and arms the size of my thighs, a round, pudgy face, pock-marked from acne, and a couple of gold teeth. He likes gold and usually wears a gaudy necklace and many large rings. He almost always wears sunglasses, no matter what time of day or year. I estimate that he has a dozen or so tattoos, mostly gang-related. The full name of his gang is inscribed in black gothic letters on his forearms and he has smaller tattoos depicting gang insignia on his neck, chest, and hands. A black teardrop tattoo, which usually signifies that the wearer has killed someone or a fellow gang member has been killed, falls from his left eye. Both sides of his head are buzz cut with a stripe of slightly longer hair down the middle. He often preens his Mohawk, smoothing the raised middle part or kneading it with gel. He reminds me of a skunk strutting down the sidewalk. Perhaps I'm biased. He has been involved in two police standoffs in which he barricaded himself and his hostages inside a house surrounded by SWAT teams. He seems to enjoy his notoriety almost as much as his Mohawk.

Kim suffered a beating by other male gang members as an initiation ritual. But because of her friendship with Kenny, it was rather a minor affair, nothing compared to what new recruits usually have to endure. From that point on, the men in the gang gave her much respect. In fact, some feared that they would be subject to Kim's violence. They went out of their way to welcome her and provided lots of opportunities for her to make money.

By the time she was fourteen, Kim was heavily involved in her gang. She was convicted again of auto theft and also joy riding, break and enters, aggravated assault, and assault causing bodily harm. She was in and out of foster homes.

She laughed when she told me the story of how she met her younger brother and biological mother. Handcuffed and on her way to court, she was placed in the van with other inmates, both youth and adults. "I fucking ran into her and my younger brother while in the court van! I had not seen Chris, my brother, in so many years. I had never met my mom. And there she was. We were all in handcuffs going to court. And I met my fucking mom!" Of course, Kim had lived with her mother briefly when she was six, but she had not known that the woman was her mother. She overheard a woman introducing herself to another offender and immediately picked up on her name.

When Kim introduced herself, her mother said, "I've been looking for you for a long time." Kim knew this was a lie. She had seen this woman, her mother, at her grandmother's place before. Her mother knew who she was but had never bothered to say hello.

Chris had been staying with their mother, who had introduced him to intravenous drugs. While her brother was appearing in court to face a second-degree murder charge (he subsequently got off, although in Kim's mind he was guilty because he was present when the murder went down), her mother was in for armed robbery.

Kim remembered taking on a mothering role with her own biological mother when they were both in jail; Kim was in a secure facility for youth and her mother was in an institution for women. "My mom asked me for help when we were both in jail. It was kind of weird. She was being beat up by girls and chicks. I told those chicks in my letters to leave her alone." Although her biological mother had never had anything to do with Kim, all of a sudden she was asking Kim to take care of her in prison. The irony was not lost on Kim.

✳ ✳ ✳

The leadership in Kim's gang did not plan on having women in positions of power. In their minds, women were sex toys and girlfriends, often relegated to working the street; they could not be relied on to think but were inanimate objects, existing for the pleasure of men. So Kim was a curious beast to them. She was tough, loyal, and smart. She was not going to be bullied or made to do things she did not want to do. Although the leaders would never admit it, other members of the same gang told me that the leaders were afraid of her. They had never met a woman so independent and strong-willed.

Kim was one of the few girls recognized as legitimate gangsters with soldiers working directly under them. Although other women were involved in the gang, they all had to work the streets to pay off their drug debts. They always owed money because they were always injecting morphine and cocaine. "They [the higher-ups] would tell you to get out there and sell your fuckin' ass."

Kim didn't know why the senior members trusted her to carry large amounts of money and drugs or why she was placed in such an important position in the gang. "I dunno why they trusted me with this shit. Like, why wouldn't you put my fuckin' ass walkin' the streets, you know? That's the thing: I think I was a lot smarter than a lot of people." Some girlfriends of male gangsters would have to clean gang houses in their underwear because their boyfriends did not trust them not to steal drugs. "And these were their girlfriends, Mark," she told me. "And nobody would ever say anything in front of the other guys, and I was wondering why shit was the way it was."

The gang hierarchy was rigid and people had to stay within the boundaries of their role. There was one president, one vice-president, four captains, some higher-ups, many soldiers or strikers, and the new recruits.

Kim is fond of looking back at the good old days with her gang and making comparisons to gang life today. "Back then, we had certain rules. There were expectations and we had respect for each other. There was a reason for doing things. We had certain ways of going about things." Intravenous drug use by junior members was not permitted. The founders of the gang, however, were all addicts and as such, they permitted themselves to slam (inject drugs). There was violence, but murders were not that common. Things were very organized. Kim told me, "there are no rules. Things are not organized. You get killed over nothing. We had lots of guns when I was involved, like sawed off shotguns. But I was scared of them. I would not want to touch them. I was so nervous."

Kim's biological mother started working the streets as a young teen. This likely had something to do with Kim making the choice not to be a sex trade worker. The fact that both her biological parents were addicts also influenced her decision never to do hard drugs. Although Kim struggled with her self-identity, she knew what she did not want to be like: her own parents. She knew the ropes from a young age. "No one ever told me to get out there and sell my ass. Why not put my ass on the fucking street? Because I was a lot smarter. I did not have an addiction. I was not working to get drugs. This changed the way my higher-ups looked at me."

Because Kim was not addicted, she did not have to pay back drug money to the gang. For this reason, she never had to work the streets. Instead, she got other girls hooked on morphine and crack, let them build up a drug debt, and then forced them into prostitution. If they did not do it voluntarily, she would beat them senseless. Kim would meet younger girls and offer them crack and powder cocaine. She would get them doing lines and buying weed from her. She had the gig down to a science. She would start them with drugs one week, then gradually get them on the harder drugs: from marijuana to coke, crack, then needles. She would keep track of how much money they owed, get them addicted so they would need a continuous supply, and then without the means to pay her back, they had to work the street. There was no profit margin: Kim took all the money they earned. When they refused to work or hand over the money, she hurt them until they gave in. Kim told me that this was "just business." She had to turn over a large chunk of this money to her higher-ups in the gang and wanted to have money left over for herself.

Kim told me that she had women many years older than herself working for her. At first, she was not taken seriously because of her age: she was fourteen and fifteen, making thirty-year-olds work the sex trade. Kim was afraid. "I was fucking scared. Go up to a thirty-five-year-old street woman and ask her to give you her own money. I had to fight her and she was not going to listen to a fourteen-year-old girl. After a while they just paid it. I was the one who would be there every week." Some she had met years earlier at her father's place, when they were doing needles with him and buying drugs from him. "Now they had to answer to me after all those years. I was the boss. Downtown, in the hood, they had to pay me, answer to me. All their money had to come to us. I was the only one who was sober. They paid me a taxing fee and then we were the ones with the drugs." What Kim meant was that if women were going to work in the turf claimed by her gang (which was pretty much the whole downtown core and the hood), they had to pay up.

Sometimes she did not have to initiate the girls into working the street. The gang higher-ups had already set some of the older women up — they were already addicted and knew they had to turn their money over. In these cases, Kim had only to collect the money from them every couple of days.

"Because I was the only one who didn't do it, I realized things that others did not. This was the only reason I did not shove a needle in my arm." Kim was terrified that she would catch Hepatitis C or AIDS from her girls. She understood that if her blood mixed with theirs, she would be at high risk of contracting such illnesses. "Back then, there were no cleaning kits or needle exchange programs. Rigs were full of shit. This one friend of mine would get into the yellow pail of sharps that nurses had. He'd use dirty needles and he got AIDS." I asked her if she ever talked about safe sex with her girls. She never did. She also told me that she never knew if her girls made their tricks (men who paid them for sex) use condoms.

Kim told me that she was remorseful for doing all these terrible things to women, but she believed that her feelings could not change the fact that she preyed on young women and used violence to get them to do whatever she wanted. When discussing this, Kim's body posture changed considerably. She slumped down in her chair, made no eye contact, and hid her face in her hands. Her voice tremored slightly; I could tell that she was close to tears.

Kim profited tremendously from trafficking cocaine and forcing girls to work the street. She was able to make a good living because she steered clear of drugs and was widely respected both within the gang and on the streets. "When I joined, it was friggin' fun. I sold lots of drugs. But all my higher-ups were using drugs and were high all the time. I never used. Because they were out of it they would trust me, give me all their drugs and money. I ended up selling not only my drugs but theirs too."

Many times Kim bailed out her gang bosses. Because of their addictions, they would blow all the money that was supposed to be turned over to their higher-ups. They would put the squeeze on Kim for the money. "Sometimes I felt threatened by my higher-ups. They did not have enough money to cover their own fuck-ups, like blowing it all on drugs. The problems were passed down the line; there was always someone who had to pay." Although Kim felt this was unfair, she would bail them out and in turn earned their respect so they would have her back if shit ever came down from her enemies on the streets and in other gangs. If Kim did not have enough money, she forced the gang members under her to give her the money.

Kim was on her way to developing a gang identity: "I was a somebody. It was the way people looked at me. They were afraid of me and knew I was good for business. I brought in a fuck of a lot of money." Kim made between $4,000 and $5,000 a month, depending on how good business was. But she was not rich. She did not have a bank account and spent the money as soon as she had it.

Kim prided herself on the fact that she never disclosed to anyone that she was bailing people out — that she never ratted on anyone. Even when faced with hard time in jail, she never cut a deal for a lesser sentence. She could have taken the whole gang down. Instead, she shut her mouth and did her time. Because of Kim, many other senior gang members never had to do any time. She took responsibility for many of their crimes. "I did not rat on anyone. If I was a dumb, naive sixteen-year-old I could have taken down everybody. I didn't. That changed the way they looked at me."

Over a period of two years, Kim established a cocaine distribution network inside some correctional facilities. She sent dealers into facilities to visit inmates and provide them with drugs. She recruited a few guards to bring drugs to inmates as well. Kim also collected money from drug deals set up by higher-ups who were too out of it to do it themselves.

At age sixteen, Kim was charged with two counts of organized crime and twenty-two other offenses related to kidnapping, drug trafficking, and prostitution. Three other gang members were convicted of organized crime along with Kim. They ended up serving sentences of approximately five years each.

Kim began to think of leaving gang life while she was serving time for her convictions. Her grandmother called her, crying a few times, upset that she was not able to see her. Kim had heard that fellow gang members on the street were being killed off by a splinter cell, a small group of gang members that left the original gang to form their own gang. Kim did not believe it at first. She could not see how a smaller, relatively new gang could threaten her gang, which was large and well-organized.

"When I got out they took a bat to me. I got rolled by these guys. I was really scared. I was a big name getting out of jail and they wanted it known that they were serious. They put me in the hospital. I had stitches and everything."

After the splinter cell beat Kim, she was paranoid for a long time. She knew where these gangsters lived, and they knew where she lived. Her younger brother was on house arrest, and Kim said that he was paranoid as well. He left knives all around the house, just in case they got rushed by this rival gang. "That gang went on to kill a lot of my friends. I felt like people were dropping like flies."

Kim lost four close friends in one summer to shootings, stabbings, and overdoses. Many others did not die but suffered serious injuries from these attacks. "At this party, my friend Charlie got stabbed in the heart. I seen him fall on the floor, take his last breath. I remember just going out the back door and running all the way back to my grandma's house. And I remember I was pacing on the porch, back and forth and back and forth. I said to myself that I cannot do this anymore."

Soon after this murder, Kim took ecstasy with another friend, Andie, one of the founders of her gang. Kim had never done chemicals before. They were up for days and days. He was also doing morphine, though Kim didn't know this. He overdosed — she tried to use CPR on him and called for help. When the police arrived, he was dead. Andie was a captain and other gang members blamed Kim for his death. They believed that she did not do enough to help him although she did what she could.

Kim told me, "I did not want to die. I was so tired of it." She had lost many fellow gang members and friends in such a short period of time and was sick of the life. She never had the chance to properly grieve these losses. As well, she wanted to have a child and did not want her son or daughter to experience what she had gone through.

Due to her close friendship with Kenny, Kim had a relatively easy exit from the gang. Over the next two or three years, Kim stayed friends with her higher-ups. She partied with them and went to gang meetings. But that was the extent of her involvement. After she left the gang she worked to complete high school and was working on and off at part-time jobs. She also began to attend the gang project where I met her. Many of her friends had been in the same project and despite having left the life for a while, most were back into gangs and heavily addicted. One of the hardest things she ever had to do was make peace with the members of the rival gang that killed her friends. Many of them were participants in the gang project. This required her to "look people in the face when I knew that they fuckin' killed somebody. That they killed my friends. And learning how to fuckin' feel for that person you know — even if that person killed my friend, there is a reason why he was like that."

It is late fall 2012 when we last sit down to catch up on things. We have not spoken for about seven months. Kim gave birth to a baby boy exactly one year ago and she has just returned from shopping for his birthday party. I'm eager for her to tell me about what she's been up to, especially about being a first-time mother.

Jimmy is big for a one-year-old, weighing in at about thirty pounds. Kim feels that he has given her a new chance on life: an opportunity to break the cycle of abuse, addiction, and abandonment that characterized her family while she was young. As a single parent, life has been challenging. She still has few supports. But, "For the first time in my life I feel normal, with a baby and a house. I never had that before. I have this kid who loves me unconditionally. And he is happy to see me. I never had that before, to take pride in. When I was pregnant I said to myself, 'I don't want to fuck this up, I don't wanna fuck this up.'" Kim is proud that Child and Family Services have not taken Jimmy away. She keeps pinching herself because this is new territory for her. "I raise him by myself and he is mine," she crows. "Those fuckers will never take him away from me."

The father of her baby is older than Kim by five years or so. He is of little help and Kim kicked him out because he physically abused her and is an addict. "He is a mean drunk. Once he smashed the door in. He tried to hit me often." Kim went to a women's shelter for one week, got legal aid, and had her own place shortly thereafter. She doesn't understand why he doesn't take responsibility for his actions or his son. "His mother is the cause of some of his problems." He doesn't provide any financial support, despite having a well-paying job. "He drinks and does blow every weekend." He lives just a couple of blocks away but sees the baby only if they bump into one another in the community or at a mall. "If I had a choice I would never see him again — he's a loser bitch dumbass." Kim and I talked about why she stayed with this man for so long. Kim told me that she longed for a perfect family — a husband, kids, and a nice house. This prevented her from seeing the impact of his violence and addictions.

Things have not been easy. She has felt alone and powerless at times. Noni and her boyfriend have been living with her for the past year. Her grandmother starts drinking as soon as her feet hit the floor in the morning "and she is drinking and drinking and drinking." Her boyfriend does needles. Noni criticizes Kim constantly and cannot be trusted to look after the baby. "I feel like she thinks I am not a good mother. She is always calling me down." Yet, Kim is able to see why Noni is so hard on her. Noni has lots to worry about. Her children are all addicts and have lived on the streets.

Kim's mother died in 2008 at the age of thirty-eight. Kim was twenty-one. "Her heart was older than her body. She worked the street her whole life. It was a heart attack from drug use." Her father is very ill from years of intravenous drug abuse.

Kenny tried to infiltrate the project in its last year of operation. The staff team believed that he posed a serious threat to their safety and that of the program participants. More than once he ordered some of his soldiers to infiltrate the program, posing as ex-gang members who needed help in order to gain information on who was in the program, the identities and contact information of staff, and the building layout. He wanted to know how the security system worked and where the cameras were on the inside of the building. He was, for the most part, successful in gathering this intelligence. Three of his soldiers managed to get accepted into the program, but they stayed only long enough to figure out who was doing what. Staff members finally implemented an intake process whereby potential candidates were carefully screened off-site and accepted into the program only once their motivation for joining was clear. Kenny eventually entered the program himself, albeit under strict conditions, in the last year, but staff believed that his intentions for leaving the gang were suspect. Shortly after being accepted into the program, he ripped off one of his higher-ups — the word on the street was that he owed $40,000. He left town on the run.

Kim wants to plan for her future. She wants a career. But she does not want to leave her baby with anyone, largely because she is worried he will be neglected and abused. She has tried to leave him with family and friends while looking for a job, but this did not work out: "He just flipped out." There are two things she is proud of in her life: the baby and the fact that she completed the anti-gang project. But now the program has been shut down and Kim has nowhere to go for support. She says, "I need to find my own way. I need something for myself." Almost all her friends are in prison, in witness protection, addicted, or active gang members. Thinking about the amount of money she used to make, she now says she should have saved and made a down payment on a house or paid for her son's schooling.

Reflecting back on her years in the gang, Kim is very insightful. She is clear on why she joined and what the gang gave her. "You know, Mark, I felt out of place when I was in that first foster home. Then I went to that new school. They all knew that I was in foster care. I felt embarrassed. The other students wanted to know why. I did not know myself. I just wanted to get the fuck out of there. When I was in the gang, I felt like I fit in, I was taken care of, they had my back. I did not feel alone. And there was lots of racism at that school. The foster family was all white too. I can't say that I knew what it meant to be Aboriginal back then. I did not know."

Kim has since taken part in many cultural activities and is very proud of her Cree roots. About five years ago, she met a female Elder who spoke Cree and very little English. The anti-gang project introduced the Elder to the participants in the hope that they would learn about their roots and develop a cultural identity, which could replace their gang identity. Although apprehensive at first, Kim slowly began to trust this woman. The Elder taught Kim how to bead and a few words in Cree. Kim and other participants went to powwows and round dances. Occasionally they went to sweat lodges. Slowly, as Kim distanced herself from gang life, she grew to respect the Elder, and took pride in her cultural traditions.

Kim and I converse over Facebook frequently. She is okay. When we last talked in person, I asked her to tell me the one biggest reason why she got involved in gang life. Without hesitation, she said: "I did not know who I was. That's why, Mark."

✳ CHAPTER 2 ✳

JESUS DON'T WORK FOR ANYONE

Terrence's suit barely fits him. He's over six feet tall and weighs more than 200 pounds. His neck and trapezius muscles bulge, and he can barely lift his arms — his "pipes" — up over his head because his jacket is nowhere near big enough to house them. His shoulders look so much wider than a typical doorway that he likely has to go through some sideways. His forearms and wrists are covered with old scars from cigarette burns and from cutting himself with a knife or razor. He twitches constantly.

His hair is tightly curled and short; he's clean-shaven but has a long scar running down the right side of his face, from his cheekbone to the corner of his mouth. His nose is flat and sags: evidence of too many fights. He has a deep, husky voice and his head is huge. These are well-known signs of long-term steroid abuse.

I've known Terrence since he was fifteen years old, when his adoptive mother, Valerie, called the youth agency where I worked wanting help with her "out of control" son. Over the next twenty years or so, I followed his criminal career through the media. Although he was by no means always in the spotlight, he made the news a couple of times each year. Then, through an odd coincidence — the coach of my daughters' rugby team was dating his sister Nancy — we caught up again. He lived a life of rejection and alienation and sought to be understood.

Terrence came from mixed-race biological parents, probably African and Caucasian, although there were no official records of this. He and his biological sister, June, suffered significant neglect from their birth parents. They were fed pizza crusts for meals and had very little physical contact with adults — they were neither hugged nor even touched. They often spiraled into violent tantrums, flailing their arms and legs wildly and screaming uncontrollably.

When Terrence was three and June was six, they were adopted by a mixed-race couple, Valerie and James, who had two older children of their own, Chris and Nancy. They lived in an affluent area of town, in a large, two-story brick house on a quiet street lined with maple trees.

Terrence's early childhood in his adoptive home — in his memory, at least — was idyllic: "My early years were the most glorious time of my life. I had everything that a kid could want and need." But Terrence also flip-flopped in his accounts of early life: one minute he was in Disneyland, the next he was humiliated and crying in a corner of his room.

Valerie was well-connected with the political elite, both at the municipal and provincial level, and was on the Board of Directors of a local non-profit social agency where she was always helping others. She aided refugees who came to the city, volunteered on political campaigns, and found the time to be a full-time teacher at a local school. She was also a "functioning alcoholic," a term Terrence learned in an Adult Child of Alcoholics support group he once attended.

Terrence adored his adoptive father, even though he was very strict and temperamental. James, a senior manager at a large international company, was athletic and charismatic, but his good looks masked a nasty streak, which erupted periodically towards those who were closest to him. "He was the epitome of a provider for sure. He berated and chastised us to instill fear."

Neither his adopted family nor the Children's Aid Society social worker could give Terrence a straight answer about where he and June came from. "Like, hearing from my mother that I am from Barbados and [of] Asian descent, and from my sister that I am Jamaican, and my social worker didn't know." Being adopted made his origins even more uncertain. "It was at a young age that I realized I was adopted and I was different from other kids. When I was first adopted I kept asking my mom 'When am I gonna turn white?' I thought my skin colour would change."

When they were kids, Terrence's older brother, Chris, was into martial arts and used Terrence as a punching bag. When he was six, Chris made Terrence watch *The Many Faces of Death* over and over again. This stomach-churning DVD of actual suicides, homicides, beheadings, and other real-life deaths helped desensitize him to violence. June was tough as nails and she and Terrence scrapped often, egged on by Chris and Nancy. "I learned to fight at home." His older siblings told him "don't be a tattletale and tell Mom and Dad." Invariably, Terrence would be blamed for the fights, which usually resulted in a "whooping" from dad.

His parents split up when Terrence was about eight years old. Valerie was already having an affair with Ralph, the man who then became Terrence's new stepfather. Terrence "hated him from day one." James had also had affairs during the marriage, though Terrence didn't know that then. "I lost my breath when they first talked about separation. I thought they were perfect."

Although Terrence idolized his older brother, he now believes that Chris turned him into a predator. Terrence told me that he felt humiliated when Chris used to beat him up, and consequently he made a decision early on in life that nobody else would ever do that to him again. "I was a complete fireball with inner rage and turmoil and dysfunction."

Racism and discrimination were behind some of Terrence's rage. Apart from his siblings and James, he was the only black person in the region. He was teased incessantly in primary school. He learned to fight back. In grade three, he was suspended for fighting a bigger kid who was much stronger than he was. All he wanted was to be liked and accepted. Instead, he was earning a reputation as a crazy, tough kid who was not to be messed with. He wanted power and respect, but understood early that his colour presented a major challenge to getting this.

Once, he brought a pig's head to his elementary school. He cut out the pig's brain and ran around with it in his hand to terrorize the other students. He also cut off the pig's nose and bit it. At the same time, he was a sensitive child who craved the attention of the kids he was alienating. He got that attention by scaring the pants off them.

In grades six and seven, Terrence continued to fight other students and got suspended many times as a result. "I became somewhat of a bully here and there." And although he was placed in classes for gifted students, he did not get any help for his anger. Many mental health professionals, including a psychiatrist who was a leading expert on anti-social behaviour, assessed him. After attempting to evaluate the boy on numerous occasions, the psychiatrist gave up and told Terrence's parents that their son was "untreatable." Terrence manipulated and fooled every test that was administered and refused to engage with therapists. He learned at a young age that he could and had to outsmart adults and win at all costs. His parents stopped believing that they could help him and attributed his behaviour to bad genes. In their minds, the family environment had nothing to do with how he was turning out.

In grade nine, Terrence was again placed in the gifted class. The class size was much smaller than the regular class, and teachers thought that this would help manage his behaviour. This was a mistake. He was younger than the other students because he had skipped a grade or two. He started hanging out with an older crowd and gravitated towards students who were into drugs, alcohol, and crime. He prided himself on being cool and not ratting out other kids. He always had the best clothes and the latest rap CDs. He adopted the swagger of older boys and hung out with older girls. He also played on the football team, which was a positive experience that made his father proud. James was instrumental in helping Terrence sort out the racism and his feelings of being different. He taught Terrence to use his colour to his advantage, especially in sports. "Don't use being coloured as an excuse and a crutch," his father would say. Terrence desperately wanted his father's love, especially after his parents divorced.

Even at the top of his game, Terrence was churning on the inside, his rage was always bubbling just below the surface. He often felt like killing other people — his brother and Ralph. He felt abandoned — first by his biological parents and then by his adoptive parents. He blamed himself for their divorce. "I felt I was a bad person." He was no angel during his teen years, but deep down he just wanted the perfect family.

When Valerie couldn't handle Terrence's drug use and violent behaviour any longer, she gave him an ultimatum: leave the house and be cut off from all financial support, or go away to the boarding school on the prairies where his stepfather, Ralph, had completed his high school studies. Although Terrence was profiting from his criminal activities, he was not making enough to pay for rent and food. He didn't want to go away, though, so he contacted his adoptive dad to see if he could stay with him instead. James said that it was his idea to send him to boarding school and that he had no sympathy for Terrence's situation. This stung. Even though his dad had not had much to do with him since the divorce, Terrence still idolized him and longed for his attention. This was yet one more rejection that left him feeling even more alone and unwanted.

Terrence lasted only three months at boarding school. He gravitated towards other marginalized students who were into alcohol and drugs. He rarely went to class and completed assignments about as often as he did chores around the house — which was never. He injured his knuckles by punching the school's brick walls and had large bumps on his head from butting his head into the brick walls of his room. When he felt pain, Terrence knew he was alive. He was expelled from the school for doing magic mushrooms and cocaine, though he still denied the drug use to his mother.

Shortly after returning home, on an early evening in late November, Terrence, armed with a machete, robbed a local store. The police had an easy time apprehending him: they simply followed tracks in the newly fallen snow and knocked on the door of the house where they led. A pair of boots in the front hall appeared to be the same size and tread as the footprints, and Terrence confirmed that they were his. The officers put him in handcuffs and read him his rights.

Terrence was convicted of armed robbery and assault with a weapon and was sentenced to twelve months in a secure facility. (In court, he sweet-talked the judge into giving him a lighter sentence than the one the Crown requested.) Instead of interrupting his spiraling journey into crime and gangs, incarceration had the opposite effect: Terrence bonded with other youth who were heavily involved in serious crime.

Everyone in the facility liked him. He was charming, well-spoken, and appeared to get along with the other youth just fine.

He was a master manipulator and controlled the other youth through intimidation, all under the radar of the staff. He had to be top dog and would do anything to get the respect and control over all of the other youth in the facility. "I had a good way of knowing what to say and what to do to fuck with someone big time, even if I did it belligerently to make it look like somebody else did it. My manipulation was crazy. From all the things that I had seen and felt and been through I could fuck with people, like hard-core. It was really messed up." A youth worker in the facility said, "He's gotta be the best bullshitter I have ever seen. Especially with the female staff. He has everyone thinking that he is totally into counselling, but it's all lies."

He worked out hard in the gym in the basement of the centre, by lifting heavy weights, and he gained ten pounds of muscle. He learned that he could control people with his size, without saying a word or raising a fist. He used his charm and good looks to convince everyone that he was rehabilitated.

When Terrence got out, he quickly picked up where he had left off. He was supposed to be in grade eleven at the same high school he attended before being apprehended, but he had no intention of stopping his drug dealing, robberies, or partying. He re-established himself with the same group he ran with before and also networked with other friends he had met inside the young offender facility. They formed a gang.

Terrence carved out a reputation for himself as a "bad boy" who surrounded himself with "bad chicks." These young women were good at stealing, and because they did not have a criminal record, they were unlikely to be apprehended by the police. He was the leader of what he called a "booster ring," a group of youth who stole hats and hoodies from local stores. He was a really good thief. He gave the stolen clothes to older Jamaican guys who gave him dope and beer in return. Break and enters followed. "I could get you whatever. Everyone wanted to know what I had and what I stole." This made him very popular and for once he felt accepted at school. He became an enforcer, beating up people who had debts owing for drugs or loans. "I would tell them 'You owe me fucking money.' I held all the chips." He was also dealing drugs and had no problem collecting from other youth who owed him. He spent lots of time playing poker and pool with his friends. He always bet money and usually came out ahead.

On the outside he looked all-powerful, but on the inside he was filled with pain.

Around this time, Terrence's older sister Nancy believed that June may have been sexually abusing Terrence, a topic Terrence absolutely refuses to discuss. An uncle had been abusing his own two daughters over many years; everyone in the family knew but kept this hushed up. The parents told the children not to tell anyone what was going on. As Nancy said, "We showed well. Everything was rainbows and lollipops. No one knew that inside our house there was lots of shit going on. The perfect exterior was all a façade."

It was also around this time that Terrence tried to hang himself. The sexual abuse likely had something to do with this, although I can't be certain. Terrence would not discuss why.

It was a clear day in May, about four in the afternoon, sunny but not hot. Terrence walked, carrying a rope, to a wooded area near his house. He made a noose, hung it from the tree, and placed it around his neck. He climbed up on a log and stepped off it. He was hanging, toes off the ground, when a friend found him and quickly pulled him down, saving him at the last minute.

About one week later, Terrence committed a brutal assault. A student at the high school owed drug money to his crew, so Terrence "curb stomped" him: he stomped on the back of the victim's head while holding his mouth on the curb of a road, resulting in broken teeth and a broken jaw. Terrence did this in plain view of his friends. He later told me that he felt like a train wreck, completely out of control. If he couldn't kill himself, he had to try to kill someone else.

With his gang, Terrence learned how to be a smarter criminal, but he was not quite smart enough. He landed back in the same young offender facility on a fourteen-month stint for aggravated assault, break and enter, possession of stolen property, extortion, and breach of probation. This all happened after his suicide attempt. Again, his incarceration did nothing to change his criminal ways. He spent his time talking with like-minded youth and planning with them the crimes they would commit once they were released. In reference to the assault on the schoolboy, Terrence said to me that he told staff that he was afraid of his own violence. Who knows if he was being truthful?

After getting out of the young offender centre for the second time, he became heavily involved in armed robberies and drug trafficking. This lasted for about two years until he turned twenty. He was buying kilos of coke from gang-involved suppliers and selling to customers across the city. He became notorious. "People liked me and wanted to be like me." During this time he began using steroids.

At age twenty, two years after his second round in a youth facility, Terrence began work as an independent enforcer and debt collector. He did not care which gang he worked with as long as he could dictate the terms of his work. The Triads (a Chinese organized crime group), the Crips (a mainly street gang), biker gangs, and Middle Eastern groups all used his services.

He did not want to be seen as a member of any of these gangs, but as an independent. "I have never been initiated but I have been affiliated. I've done a lot of shit for these gangs. Some people say I've been a member, but it's not true. I'm an enforcer. I don't work for anyone." No one gang was going to put their symbol on Terrence. He had no gang-related tattoos. "I was so diverse and talented. I did not feel the need to be part of any one thing. I felt better than everybody. The bikers, the Crips, were nothin'. No one had power over me. You're not gonna tell me what to do. So the Afghanis said, 'We would like you to work with us, not for us.'"

Highly organized groups like biker gangs don't take too kindly to independent operators. Because of their rigid hierarchy, it was very unusual for them to have an ongoing business relationship with someone like Terrence. But, as long as it was part of conducting his own business, Terrence had no problem getting shot at, sliced with a machete, or beaten with a steel pipe. "I don't know any fear. I've always been on top of the food chain."

One time, a guy ratted out a member of a Middle Eastern gang. Members of the gang told Terrence that the guy had "pointed the finger at us" and showed Terrence where he lived. Terrence asked, "Well, how would you like me to get this guy's finger? I'll slice it off. And I'll give you a good price" — ten grams of cocaine. Terrence went to the guy's house, held him down, and demanded to know which finger the victim used to point out the gang member to the police. The victim, thinking his life might be spared, held out the index finger of his right hand. Terrence took a pair of garden cutters from his pocket and cut the finger off.

Terrence moved in with a girlfriend. It was not a healthy relationship and was ridden with violence and drug abuse. He was cooking crack at the apartment and distributing it to other dealers, who in turn sold it on the street. He was also addicted to cocaine, which he both snorted and smoked. He was not happy about abusing his girlfriend, but he believed she threatened his manhood when she fought back instead of just sitting back and taking it. "I was jealous as fuck and felt like a loser." Drug-induced psychotic rages, fuelled by steroids and cocaine, made him feel omnipotent and in total control. But, once the drug high was over, the feelings of self-doubt and rejection re-emerged. His physical stature, largely the result of steroids and lifting heavy weights, helped balance out his negative emotions.

At age twenty-one, Terrence had a screaming fight with James about his drug use and criminal activities. Terrence came home after the fight, placed two bullets in the chamber of his handgun, spun the chamber, cocked the trigger, held it under his chin, and pulled. Click. He did it again. Click. Crying, Terrence threw the gun in the bathtub.

After this suicide attempt, Terrence experienced flashbacks to the violence at home he endured as a child. He remembered having his lip split open by a slap from Valerie when she was drunk. He remembered being strapped by James. He thought about the time he punched his stepfather in the face and then was knocked out cold by the man. He thought of what he could do differently if he had his own son, how he could be a better parent.

He began to think about leaving the gang life, but couldn't make the break. Within three months of his second suicide attempt, Terrence was back in prison for drug, weapons, armed robbery, kidnapping, and assault charges.

Terrence became a born-again Christian while serving time during this latest prison sentence and awaiting a parole hearing. The timing is peculiar: finding Jesus likely did not hurt his case and he did get early release after a lengthy stay inside. After his conversion, he maintained his reputation.

Terrence was proud of his reputation inside correctional centres: "I'm the kingpin in jail, the solid guy." He never experienced protective custody, even after he was stabbed repeatedly inside. "Someone had a hit out on me, I don't know who." The stabbing resulted in many scars all over his torso and arms as well as the nasty gash on his face.

After his release, Terrence made lots of money with his crack crew, which was based out of a large social housing complex in the eastern part of a large city in central Ontario. He ran about twenty guys. As the leader, he set up the crack houses, established the distribution network, and ensured that his boys sold a good product to their customers. It was not a gang, he stressed. He was adamant that this was an independent operation, although such operations typically were run out of town, forced to pay a tax, or beaten into joining established gangs. Terrence did not experience any of these things. "I've done so many favours, no one's going to tell me not to sell where I want." To Terrence, his altruistic behaviour on the street was like money in the bank: it allowed him to call the shots whenever and wherever he wanted. He had no problem taking out other independent dealers operating on his turf, and frequently he was called on to do the same for other groups. At the same time, he could also pull together ten to twenty members of any gang to help him out on tough cases. Whether they were Somalis, Afghanis, or guys in his own drug crew, it made no difference.

Terrence also ran prostitutes on the street. He was convicted of living off the avails of prostitution but was quick to say that he was never a pimp, though he said, "I beat up some girls pretty good." He chalked his involvement up to drugs and money. Because he "inherited" the prostitutes after running other independents out of town, he felt this was somehow not the same as forcing them to work for him. He just didn't want to talk about it.

This went on for six years. Then, when he was twenty-seven, Terrence met Sally, an African woman in her twenties, at a crack house. Sally guarded the house and kept a lookout for the cops. She also was the go-to person for a biker gang. She bought large quantities of almost-pure coke from them, had her own soldiers cut it with baking soda and dextrose to make it go longer, and put it in small Baggies. Her soldiers collected the money after runners made sales to their clients.

One day, Terrence was desperate for a fix and went to the

house, hoping for some free crack. He had heard of Sally, and she likewise knew his reputation. She gladly fronted him enough crack for the next couple of days. There was an immediate physical attraction between them, and they soon began seeing each other.

June committed suicide shortly after Terrence met Sally. Terrence says that he has no idea why she killed herself, although he revealed that her boyfriend was abusing her. They had very little contact with each other in the ten years prior to my interview with Terrence, and it is not clear to me why this was the case. He was agitated and angry when talking about her death, calling her selfish to leave her year-old child behind and with no right to take her own life; in contrast, Terrence talked about his own suicide attempts without emotion. Terrence has clearly been impacted by the suicide of June, and in the absence of any further information from him, I can only surmise that it has something to do with the sexual abuse.

Six months after Terrence and Sally began seeing each other, Sally found out she was pregnant; she quit crack cold turkey and dropped her gang involvement.

Things changed when Terrence spiraled further down into the world of crack. His habit cost him about two hundred dollars a day. He became a "slum thug" — he was so cracked out that he was unable to conduct business. The drugs overtook everything. When he did jobs, it was only to buy more crack. He didn't take on big jobs because he only wanted enough for his next fix. People started to question where his loyalties lay. He became "for hire," meaning that he was no longer his own boss. He worked for gangs, no longer with them.

Crazy with crack, Terrence took his life into his own hands for the third time: he tried to jump off a bridge. It was high above a set of rapids and the water was very shallow. Sally pleaded with him to come down off the bridge, asking him what kind of life their two-year-old son would have without his dad. After some hesitation, he did come down. Shortly after this, he claims that he quit steroids. "I had heart problems and got into real trouble because I was using Accutane and steroids at the same time." He almost died.

✳ ✳ ✳

Terrence is now "in-between" substance abuse treatment centres. He's on parole and the treatment centre where he's currently residing has some pretty tight rules about how long he can be off-site. The centre is Christian-based and operates somewhat like a cult. Terrence chose this centre because of its religious foundation. The residents are supposed to blindly follow direction, all in the name of Jesus Christ. Although Terrence is very religious and became a born-again Christian long before he landed at the facility, he doesn't like the rules, is in constant conflict with the staff and other residents, and is going to move to another centre soon.

Sally and their son Billy live on the sixth floor of a run-down apartment building; her small apartment is spotless. Billy is the spitting image of Terrence as a young boy: tall for his age and skinny. As energetic as his father, he has a shaved head and an earring in his right ear. He adores Terrence, who worships him in return.

Terrence's family has played a key role in his exit from gang life. His mother has provided unconditional support. He clearly idolizes Valerie. She survived alcoholism and recently a bout of cancer. "She is my superwoman and my number one source of support." Nancy and her boyfriend have been key allies as well. Terrence has slept on their couch many nights when he has no other place to go, and they do not judge him.

Terrence is still volatile and can be violent. A couple of years ago, Terrence had an EEG brain scan, the results of which he claimed helped explain his anti-social behaviour. His theory does hold some truth. There is a growing body of scientific evidence that brain lesions can predispose an individual to aggressive, impulsive, and violent behaviour. Substance abuse has also been linked to brain dysfunction. It is possible that Terrence suffered brain trauma as a young child, before being adopted at age three. What is not clear in the research on these matters is whether brain lesions cause violent behaviour or whether suffering brain trauma causes the lesions.

He slips back into using crack from time to time, but his family has never given up on him. Recently, he was breached for using drugs and not residing at the treatment facility. He convinced the judge that he did not need to go back to jail, that he just needed a break and would clean up his act. He said he had not been attending church and, because of that, the devil was making him do evil things. This apparently did not raise any suspicions about his mental state. He also pleaded for the judge to let him get into a detoxification centre and, in fact, he did spend two nights there.

Despite his charm, good looks, and intelligence, Terrence is still highly troubled and he may again spiral into a world of crime, drugs, and steroids. He is comfortable in this world and likes the fact that he is top dog in jail. Respect, or lack thereof, is a huge issue for him, and he has limited insight into his own behaviour and environment. He has created an image of himself — as a massive and violent independent enforcer — that has to some extent worked. He has been relatively successful in his gang work except when he gets submerged by crack cocaine. If he starts to actively use crack again, he likely will have to rely on crime to pay the bills. Given the relative ease with which he made money while affiliated with gangs, he could become involved again. He has never held a legitimate job. And Terrence admits that he still has ties to gang life. A gang, for his kidnap and torture two years ago of an independent drug dealer who refused to get off the gang's turf, owes him fifty thousand dollars. He says he doesn't want to collect on this debt, though. "It's not worth it," he tells me.

Another curious aspect of Terrence's personality is worship, both of himself and Jesus. Although all addicts are to some extent self-centred (in that they focus almost all of their energy on the next fix), he has elevated this to another level. He seems to believe that he exists on a higher moral plane than everyone else, and he believes that he is untouchable. He is charismatic and has talked his way out of many bad situations. But he is also evangelical and spreads the good word to anyone who will listen. "I believe I was delivered from bondage of my own self," he tells me. He states that Jesus, hard work, and jail time have resulted in positive personal changes, and he believes that answers to his prayers (related to exiting gangs, addiction, and crime) have been delayed but are not denied. "I will be saved, just like you."

Whether or not it was Terrence who found Jesus or Jesus who found Terrence in jail doesn't really matter. Maybe this will result in Terrence getting back on track. Or, maybe there is a part of Terrence that thinks he is Jesus.

✻ CHAPTER 3 ✻

THE GANG MOTHER

Monica is short, stocky, and strong. She cultivates a butch image: army pants, close-cropped black hair, and T-shirts that show off her tattoos. On the left side of her neck is a black, circular design reminiscent of a Celtic ring. It covers an old gang tattoo that attracted too much attention from rival gangs and the police. There's another covered-up gang tattoo on her right shoulder. It was the name of her "old family," but she had it blacked out to avoid confrontations with the cops whenever she went downtown.

She's happy to talk to an attentive listener and punctuates her speech with a laugh after every sentence or two. It's nervous laughter, like a runner false starting out of the blocks, returning only to false start another time. Although we have talked many times, this pattern of laughing continues.

Monica was born in a small prairie city, the second youngest in a large family. Both her parents were alcoholics. Her father served twenty-five years in the penitentiary for a murder "he didn't do." Her mother drank throughout all of her twenty-one pregnancies.

Monica spoke mainly Cree as a young child and didn't

understand why child welfare took her and her siblings away from her mother. Monica was only four years old. "I remember the day we were all taken away. It was a hot summer day. A blue station wagon pulls up. All of us were crying. As we are pulling away, my mom is on the ground crying. Then she is running after us." Monica hasn't seen many of her biological siblings since. She believes two brothers died: one apparently overdosed and the other flipped his car and was killed.

Monica was placed in the same foster home as her older sister, Janet, and younger brother, Jim. They all had fetal alcohol spectrum disorder. Jim was the most severely affected: he was born with a developmental problem so that his legs and arms did not grow properly and were too short for his body. He had heart problems, diabetes, and celiac disease. Janet was light-skinned and hated anyone with skin darker than hers. An attention seeker, Janet always spoke in a baby voice. She was skinny but thought she was not and was obsessed with her body image. Reluctantly, Monica found herself in the position of having to look out for her siblings at the foster home.

Monica and her siblings were fostered with a white family who operated a large farm. The foster parents had three biological children — two sons and a daughter. The children were a couple years older than Monica and her siblings. The moment the social worker drove away after dropping them off, they were told they could no longer speak Cree. The foster father, Freddy, cut off Monica's long hair and told her he had no use for "fucking Indians."

Freddy was thirty-five years old and smart. Mean, but smart. He was rather small but acted as if he were a big man. His back was hunched, his knees bowed, his neck crooked and long, his prominent belly round. He kept his salt and pepper hair short, a bit longer than a brush cut.

Along with her sister and brother, Monica lived on their

farm for many years. The wheat grew high in the summertime, and she loved playing hide and seek in it. The only way to catch someone was to look for movement in the tops of the long grass. There were also endless fields of vibrant yellow canola. Sometimes grasshoppers swarmed there. Monica called them "bugs with ants in their pants." She always felt happy when she ran through these fields on hot summer days. Egged on by the chorus of cicadas, it seemed like the whole world was laughing with her then.

Early mornings were deafening — a cacophony of animal voices: roosters, ducks, pigs, sheep, cows, and horses. Monica believed that they were sad, like her. The animals were so skinny they gulped their food. Freddy got mad when Monica gave them treats. He beat her when he caught her giving apples and carrots to the horses, corn to the cows, or table scraps to the pigs. It was as if he thought that since they would be sold for slaughter, they might as well be starved. Monica could count the ribs of the horses. Freddy was incensed with how little milk the dairy cows produced. He was even angrier when he brought pigs to auction and got only twenty-five dollars for each one.

Being on the farm meant hard work. No matter how young, the children had to milk cows, collect eggs, throw bales of hay into the barn, and shovel manure. Monica was physically exhausted all the time. She got up at about four in the morning for chores, and then she walked two miles to school. As soon as she got home, there were more chores. She felt trapped. Even though all she wanted was to curl up in a ball and sleep for days, she couldn't.

Although Jim couldn't do many chores due to his disabilities, Freddy still expected that he would do his fair share. Monica ended up taking care of most of her brother's chores at the same time as her own. She resented this. "I have regrets with my brother. Why did he have to be sick? I value work. I have nothing to do with him." Monica hated her brother. But if the work wasn't done, a beating was always just around the corner and she felt it was her role to look out for him and her sister.

The abuse was not only physical, but also sexual. It started early: the first time was on Monica's eighth birthday after the party guests had left. Freddy told her to come to the garage because he had some gifts for her. His breath reeked of garlic and raw onions, his skin of cologne. She dry-heaved. "I can't throw up when he's here. He'll make it even worse," she thought. He forced his tongue down her throat. She clenched her teeth together and told him to stop it. He kneed her in the crotch. He tried to lick her tongue and she bit him hard. She ran, but Freddy was faster. He tackled her and yanked her long hair back, like jerking the ripcord on a gas lawn mower. "You'll listen to me from now on, you squaw bitch," he hissed.

"He told me to stand there. Then he comes from behind, and rubbed himself on me, and was rubbing my breasts. I froze. What the heck is happening? Is this what big girls get at this age?" After, he told her he would kill her if she told anyone. "It was almost a daily occurrence after that." She hated it the most when he forced her to suck his penis. During these assaults, he stood upright, lowered his pants and underwear, and forced her head between his legs to lick him. He tasted like salt. When Monica gagged, he got mad at her. He often told her "this is what Indian bitches are supposed to do."

Monica started using alcohol and weed after that first sexual assault. Janet introduced her to it. She started smoking cigarettes when she was eight. Marijuana quickly followed.

It was not long after the sexual abuse started that she began questioning her sexual orientation. She had her first same-sex relationship with another girl at about age nine. She enjoyed the emotional intimacy and the occasional touching. It lasted for a couple of months.

After she had endured sexual abuse and slave-like working conditions for a year, Monica ran away for the first — but not the last — time. She was only nine years old. She knew that many of her friends at school did not have homes like hers. She was certain that not all parents hurt their kids. There had to be other families that would take care of her. She longed for her real parents but had no idea how to find them. Freddy told her that her parents were lazy drunks and had died from drinking too much. Monica never believed him. Monica was caught and brought back to the farm.

Monica tried to kill herself twice. The first time, when she was ten, she threw herself off the barn roof and landed on her head. She knocked out her front teeth, broke her nose, and smashed her skull, and suffered a concussion. "I wanted out. I was a kid." Her foster parents never told anyone about this. They kept her home from school for two weeks and when the social worker called, they told her Monica was doing great. They never took her to see a doctor, fearing that they would be fingered as abusive foster parents.

When she was eleven, she told her social worker about the physical and sexual abuse. The social worker promptly asked her foster parents if it was true. By the time Monica got home, "He was waiting for me. I got the licking of a lifetime and he raped me. He told me, 'You are only an Indian. No one will care.'" The social worker did not pursue Monica's allegations and the matter was quickly forgotten about. This failure to protect Monica from abuse likely contributed to her motivation to protect others later on in her life.

Freddy's family was Roman Catholic. Church was mandatory every Sunday. "It was the only time he put his arm around us. It was all a show. But I knew what was going to happen back home." Monica believes that Freddy used his religion to cover up the abuse. He was a respected member in the community and was actively involved in Bible study groups at the church. He was fond of quoting the Bible, saying: "He who spareth the rod hateth his son: but he that loveth him chasteneth him betimes." He also said: "Withhold not correction from the child: for if thou beatest him with the rod, he shall not die. Thou shalt beat him with the rod, and shalt deliver his soul from hell."

The beatings were relentless and severe. Freddy used bull-whips, leather belts, two-by-fours, and belts with tacks. "I got a lickin' in the morning, at school, when I got home, and when I went to bed." The worst beating occurred when she was cutting the lawn with her brother. She was in grade seven. Freddy told Monica to take Jim into the house and come right back. She had not done anything in particular to set him off. "He came running at me like a bull moose. He flipped me and smashed my head into the ground. He threw a hammer at me and it lodged in my back. My foster mom started to freak out." Her eyes were swollen shut and her face beaten beyond recognition. She was told to tell her teacher that she had fallen down. "You know, I had to grow up really young."

At the age of eleven years, she was drinking whisky, sometimes twenty-six ounces a day. She drank to kill the pain. Janet always had the connections. "She was the leader of getting me into trouble with drugs and alcohol." Monica was drunk or high every time Freddy molested her; it was the only way she could cope. Yet, her foster parents ignored her drinking and drug use. She suspected that Freddy knew about it, but he did nothing because she complied with the sexual abuse.

She was not the only one Freddy was abusing, although for a long time, she believed that she was. One day, when she was fourteen and had been suffering his assaults for six years, she caught Freddy abusing Janet. Although she was shocked, then she understood that she was not the only one to blame — her sister was to blame too (or so her thinking ran at the time).

Monica believed that she somehow was the cause of the abuse. This is not unusual for children who are being severely abused to do. Freddy got Janet pregnant when she was thirteen or fourteen. Monica was not aware of this at the time, but now she knows that Janet had an abortion and later had to get a D and C (dilation and curettage). "It messed her insides up." Jim was also being abused, although, to Monica's disgust and anger, he would never admit to it.

School was a mixed blessing. Up until grade eight, it was a haven from the chores she was forced to do on the farm: "I couldn't wait to get there." She went to a one-room schoolhouse. She was left-handed but was told that only dumb kids wrote with their left hands. She quickly learned how to use her right. But it was no picnic. She was one of the few Aboriginal kids there. She got the strap often and had to repeat grades because she was on the run frequently. When she wasn't running, she got into fights with the other students. She was routinely bullied and put down because she was "an Indian." She was frequently suspended or expelled.

Between the ages of nine and ten, Monica says she ran away fifteen times. From ten to fourteen, she ran another twenty times. She tried to take her brother and sister with her, telling them "we don't need to be here." But the abuse was not something that her siblings wanted to discuss. "We had this bond that connected us. But I was the only one at the time who talked about it." Her social worker and foster family always found her after a week or so on the run. Once she got older, Monica hitchhiked as far away from them as she could. A nice man drove her all the way to Winnipeg once. Another time she got a ride to Saskatoon from a group of teenagers. She liked the freedom hitchhiking brought her. She liked not having to do chores. But life on the street was difficult. Some people who gave her rides wanted sex in return. Monica saw nothing wrong with this — it was just something that men did to girls, and she resigned herself to it. Besides, she was good at it by that time and knew how to satisfy men quickly. When she was eventually found after each run and brought back to Freddy, the beatings got worse. Monica never thought that things could deteriorate further, but they did.

And so the abuse continued. Monica felt guilty about the sexual assaults even though she knew that what Freddy was doing was wrong. She thought she was wrecking her foster parents' marriage. She was terrified of what would happen to her if her foster mother discovered that she was having sex with Freddy. Now that her sister was doing the same thing, she was even more apprehensive. She talked with Janet about this and they agreed to never tell anyone. With the innocence of little girls, the two sisters assumed that no other foster parents would take them if they revealed that they'd had sex with a foster father.

She got pregnant in grade nine at the age of fifteen and missed many days of school. She doesn't know if Freddy was the father. He was certainly raping her, but by then she was sexually active with other young men (in addition to women). This pregnancy would finally lead to Monica's removal from Freddy's farm. The social worker was concerned about Monica's health and believed that if Monica were in a different home, her running would stop.

Monica was sent to a new foster home, along with Janet and Jim, while she was still pregnant. This time it was a good home. She stayed there for about two years. To this day she calls these foster parents Mom and Dad. They never beat her but grounded her if she behaved badly. This was a new experience — she had never been disciplined without being assaulted.

Yet, her addictions continued to spiral out of control, particularly after she gave birth at the age of sixteen and child welfare authorities immediately took her baby away. Monica suffered from postpartum depression that was triggered by the experience of losing her own parents at age four. "I didn't give a shit any more after [my baby] was taken."

The second time Monica tried to kill herself was just after the birth of her child. She experienced haunting memories of her experiences with Freddy and tremendous feelings of guilt and loss related to the placement of her baby in the foster care system. She saw suicide as the only way out. She couldn't sleep because that was all she thought about. "I wanted more for myself. I couldn't get off the merry-go-round of pain." She slashed her wrists. Her new foster parents never tried to hide the suicide attempt. They took her immediately to the hospital, where she stayed in a locked psychiatric ward for two weeks. Throughout her teens, Monica also burned herself on her arms many times with cigarettes.

At sixteen, Monica smoked a "fatty" (a large joint) multiple times a day. She would wake up in the morning, drink a six-pack of beer, smoke a couple joints, and have some hash oil. At lunch and at night she repeated this pattern. She went to bed at 3 a.m. and got up for school a few hours later. Her sister was into acid. They were both alcoholics. Monica sold drugs at school and used the money to buy more drugs and alcohol.

Monica made no connection between the sexual abuse and her addictions. "Sure, I could have said no, but she [Janet] was the main reason [that I got addicted]. My sister told me smoke this, smoke that, try a beer. Then it was harder drugs."

At age seventeen Monica committed such a serious crime of violence that she was tried as an adult. I can't describe the crime because she could be identified as a result. Normally, youth who are convicted of crimes stay in the young offender system. Not Monica. Her incarceration at seventeen marked the end of her time with her new, better foster parents. By the time she was eighteen, she had started an all-female gang in the penitentiary.

Before she was released at the age of twenty-one, she contacted some male friends who were looking to start up a criminal group on the streets. Monica was searching for belonging, and her involvement in gang life was almost inevitable, given Freddy's violence. "The abuse set me up to be a gang member. I had so much hatred towards people. Gang leaders can pick up on anger issues: the look on my face, how I was caring for myself. They feed on your negativity. They are like psychologists and doctors. They can pick up on it right away."

When Monica was released from prison her male friends agreed to use the gang name from Monica's all-female gang for their new gang. She never got beaten into the gang, nor did she get gang-raped in. Yet, she herself beat new recruits into the gang when told to do so and also witnessed many gang rapes. Although these experiences were frightening, she desperately wanted to belong. "I just came out of the Pen. I had no one. I needed someone."

Monica was the only one of her siblings who got pulled into a life of gangs and crime, despite being the one who basically raised her brother and took care of her sister. Janet relied on Monica to care for her many illnesses, starting at about age twenty-two when she had a hysterectomy, and then when she had a series of strokes, heart attacks, and seizures. "I have been her mother ever since she had her first operation at age twenty-two. I get instant migraines when I see her. If I had a choice I would not talk to her at all. She annoys me." Monica's experience as a mother for her siblings shaped her and then translated into her role as mother in the gang. In reality, Monica took on a caregiver role with her siblings when they were first placed in foster care.

Within a couple of years, the gang pretty much controlled the gun and drug distribution and sex trade in a few cities in northern Saskatchewan, Alberta, and Manitoba. It had one main rival on the streets, but many rivals, including Indian Posse and the Manitoba Warriors, inside correctional facilities.

Monica returned to school when she was twenty-six years old. She was still in the gang and school did not last long. She dropped out because she was drunk all the time and was also experiencing health problems related to diabetes.

Her gang experience was unique. She was one of the few girls who never worked in the sex trade, mostly because she had a hair-trigger temper and was a stereotypical "butch" lesbian. The gang members never gave her a hard time about being lesbian, probably because they thought she would kill them if they did. They also respected her because she helped start the gang. She instilled fear into fellow gang members because of her size and her reputation as one who never backed down.

She was conflicted about sex. When with a man, she re-experienced the abuse by Freddy as if she were a child again. Memories flooded back. She could not see men as anything but perverted pedophiles who should be killed. She hated men and could not stand to be intimate with them. But Monica wanted her own children.

Monica had four children. After her first was taken away at birth, the rest were born into her gang. Their fathers knew that she was not into men. "I told them that I got pregnant but I don't like guys." She was drunk each time she had sex with the fathers of her children and had sex with each man only once. They all knew about her sexual orientation, except for one who died soon after his child was born. None of the fathers ever met his child. Monica told them that she didn't like them but she wanted kids. "My foster father destroyed my faith in men. I decided right then and there that I would never love a man. That didn't mean that I wouldn't have my own kids. It just meant that the fathers of my kids would never be involved in my life or theirs." According to Monica, not knowing their father was never a problem for her kids.

Of her three children born into the gang, all were in foster homes for most of their childhood and youth. At first she saw nothing wrong with raising her children in gang life. She harboured gangsters in her home. At one point the leader of her own gang took over Monica's house and used it as his base for directing gang activity. This lasted for almost two years. "For a while I was a pretty shabby parent. I was strung out and told anyone, 'You can take my kid.' Could be murderers. You know, you don't give a shit."

But, as the years progressed and Monica slowly came to realize that gang life was destroying her family, she changed tack. She took back control when the gangster living in their home was incarcerated on a murder charge. "My kids should never have been in a gang. I allowed gangsters to come into my home. I know it was wrong and I did have a choice. I still kick myself in the ass and ask 'Why?'" She claims her kids were never harmed. "I told people, 'You harm my kid, I'll get you back.'"

Monica was in her late twenties when Freddy was arrested and put on trial for sexual assault, not only because of his actions towards her and her siblings, but also because of how he treated his three biological children. His son, a son-in-law, and a neighbour were also convicted in what the judge called a pedophile ring. At the trial, Freddy was a different man than the one who had abused her: he was very thin, he was confined to a wheelchair, his hands and arms were trembling, and his face was hollowed and caved in. She spat in his face when she encountered him being wheeled into the courthouse by his wife. This time it was her chance to hiss in his ear: "I hope you rot in hell, you sick bastard. I'd cut your prick up in little pieces and feed it to your pigs if I could!" Although she had spent years thinking about how she would pay Freddy back for all the pain he caused her, in the end he was too ill to serve time. Monica forgave Freddy at the time of his death. "He probably did those things because he got treated that way when he was young. He'll get what's coming to him. Let God deal with him."

Whenever Monica saw a story about sexual assault on the

news, she would shake uncontrollably and weep for hours. She joined several sexual abuse survivors' groups and tried to get Janet to join too. She refused. When Monica broached the topic of forgiving Freddy, her sister flew into a rage and knocked her unconscious.

Starting at the age of twenty-seven, Monica ran a gang house for fifteen years and became, in effect, a gang mother. "As a gang mother I provided safety, I kept secrets, and I had my own set of restrictions for gang members I took care of." Safety involved taking care of members who got beaten up as well as keeping potential victims safe from harm by hiding them in her house. Secrecy meant not talking about crimes she knew were being committed — including home invasions, robberies, and gun trafficking. It also meant hiding gang members from rivals and from the police. Restrictions were a set of ethics that she believed should frame gang activities, particularly when it came to violence. Rules included not doing crimes in front of kids, men not hitting women, and not being a rat. She, herself, never hit a woman but would beat up men who did so.

What does a gang house look like? A fellow social worker visited Monica when she was an active gang mother and described the living conditions to me. Monica lived in a townhouse on a cul-de-sac in a housing project located in a marginalized neighbourhood of a medium-sized prairie city. The house served as a distribution centre for morphine and cocaine. It was filthy and reeked of urine, body odour, and rotting garbage.

There were at least fifteen gangsters, mostly male, and five or six young children, living there. Bodies were strewn on mattresses and foam pads packed on the floors of the kitchen, dining room, hallway, and bedrooms. There were no bed frames, not even for the children. It was almost impossible to reach the bathroom because every available inch of floor space was occupied. The toilet was plugged with at least one full roll of paper. Someone had tried to use a plunger and left it, still full of feces and water, on its side by the tub. The seat was hanging, attached by one screw at the back, and the lid leaned up against the tub. Both had been white at some point, but were now a grimy brown. Cockroaches scurried into the drain when the light was turned on.

Walls were pocked with holes. Kitchen cupboards were bare and without doors. Most of the chairs and the table were broken, as were the drawers whose handles were either missing or hanging on by a loose screw. There were no light fixtures, and the shadows cast by the bare bulbs were harsh, softened somewhat by the lack of paint on the walls. It was as if the light of the bulbs was sucked into the dirty walls and swallowed whole. A *National Enquirer* was rolled up and wedged under one leg of the table. On the table were a postage scale, syringes, cocaine powder, and small Baggies along with boxes of cornstarch and baking soda.

Monica didn't get into hard drugs until her early thirties. She didn't start smoking crack and injecting cocaine and morphine earlier because she didn't want to owe anything to her gang. If she did, she would have been forced into working the street to pay off her drug debts. She was constantly pressured by her associates in the gang to prostitute herself. Instead, she worked off her marijuana and alcohol debts by being a "driver" and a "runner." Being a driver entailed picking up and dropping off drugs, driving higher-ups to gang meetings and bringing them home (she was not allowed to attend meetings), and bringing associates out to reserves so they could tag houses and buildings with gang graffiti. The graffiti identified gang turf and was also used to communicate with fellow gang members and those in rival gangs. As a runner, Monica dropped off drugs to customers. Later, she moved up the hierarchy and was directly involved in selling drugs and bringing the money back to her higher-ups. She reloaded needles with cocaine and morphine and sold them back to people. She had no idea that reusing needles would expose customers to HIV and other blood-borne illnesses.

Selling forty "points" a night usually meant earning a profit of $200. Points (syringes with drugs in them) usually sold for $20, and Monica typically bought them for $10 each. Of the $400 she earned each night, roughly $200 had to be handed over to the gang leaders. She banked the remaining $200 if she did not have debts to pay off. If she did, more money had to be turned over. She was allowed to "front" points to good customers, that is, she would not demand payment immediately. But, if they didn't pay up in a couple of weeks, the enforcers in the gang would collect from them. This involved taking possessions from the customer — televisions, cars, stereos, and alcohol — or beating them up.

When Monica first began using hard drugs, a fellow addict, usually male, would "fix" her. This meant tying a rope or bungee cord around her arm, finding a vein, and sticking the needle in. One time, she "lit up like a carousel" and stopped breathing. She was taken by ambulance to emergency, where a doctor told her that she was lucky to have survived. She cleaned up for a while but then got back into drugs just as seriously. "I had dark circles under my eyes. I lost a ton of weight. I was killing myself."

When she turned thirty-five, Monica again returned to school and this time completed grade twelve. However, by then she was using hard drugs and drinking daily.

Monica was a gang mother not only to members of her own gang, but also to members of other gangs. "When I was a member of the gang, the young ones called me mom. I had thirty people in my house; about one third were under fifteen years old." The twelve- and thirteen-year-olds, who were in training to be gangsters, were on the run from child welfare and youth justice facilities. "At first, I never let the police in."

In later years, however, something changed. "I must have had a conscience because I would tell them 'If you run away, I'm phoning the cops on you.' Kids ran to my place but they would not run away from Monica." Not only was she helping the authorities to find kids on the run, she began sheltering kids from all gangs. "My rule was that you don't bring it in my house. You leave your colours at the door and you come into my house as people, not gang members." Monica claims that parents never came to her house to find their kids. The kids liked Monica, they needed a parent, and she had created an environment that was conducive to talking about their problems, hopes, and fears. "If not at my house, they would have gone to someone else's house. At least I could keep them safe here."

More than twenty years passed before Monica saw her child who was snatched from her when she was sixteen. Monica found her address on the Internet when she was eighteen but it was another five years before they met.

The gang house Monica ran was condemned by public health officials just about the time Monica was leaving gang life, and someone set it on fire before the city could tear it down. Monica now lives in a well-kept townhouse, which she keeps very clean. It has no resemblance to her previous home and is a source of great pride for her. She lives with her girlfriend, some extended family members, and various street youth who periodically stay in the house.

Monica's perception of motherhood was complicated. Who was her mother? Was it her biological mom? She hadn't seen her since the age of four. Or was it her first foster mother? To this day, Monica thinks that woman never believed that her husband was sexually abusive. She liked her second foster mother and called her Mom but lived with her for only two years.

Monica's role as a mother was also complicated. She was a mother to her children, despite the fact that they were all, at some point, taken away from her and placed in foster or group homes for extended periods of time. She realizes now that she made serious mistakes with her children. She was also forced to be a mother to her two siblings, both of whom had serious health problems.

Perhaps her gang mother role was in part a reflection of the chaotic "mothering" in other aspects of her life. It was one of the few choices she had — to be a gang mother.

Loss is a central feature of Monica's life. Her two dead brothers are not the only people she has mourned. She was separated from fourteen siblings (not including the two who died). She never saw her biological parents after she was taken away at age four. She lost her childhood to Freddy's abuse. Her first child was taken away at birth and the others were taken into foster care for many years. Many of her grandchildren have been taken away and placed in the child welfare system.

Her eldest daughter, the one who was taken away at birth when Monica was sixteen, is now twenty-eight years old, works as a waitress, and has a family of her own. They talk over the phone on holidays. Monica's other two girls are twenty-six and eleven; her son is twenty-one. Recently, Monica and another relative were put in jail on a second-degree murder charge and the youngest daughter was taken away by child welfare. However, the charge was dropped, Monica and her relative were released, and the daughter has returned home.

Monica says she has been clean and sober for the past twelve months, although she has a couple of beers on the weekends, usually after bowling with friends. For her, beer doesn't count as alcohol because it takes too many to get drunk. Although she has been out of the gang for eleven years, the responsibilities of being a gang mother have not ended. Members of various gangs crash at her place most nights, but they have to leave their gang colours and paraphernalia at the door. Their guns and drugs are usually stashed under porches of other homes or in bushes.

Many of her friends — people she has known for twenty-five years — are still involved. She raised some of these young people as if they were her own children and won't cut off ties with them. "I associate. Gangs still talk to me. I don't deal drugs, but I will still give the gang handshake." At times she is a rat, telling police about serious crimes that are being committed by gang members known to her.

Monica is constantly getting pressured to turn her home back into a haven for her original gang. She tells them that they're welcome to stay with her for a while, but that she's not a member any more. She questions them about their allegiances. "I tell them, 'Why are you still in, what does it do for you?'" She believes she has a lot to offer them: her own experience as well as community resources to help them get out of the life. "I hate to see people hurt now. I should be considered a rat in my own gang, because I keep people safe." When she was mothering gang members, it never occurred to her that one day she would be actively supporting members to exit their gangs.

Although the drugs and quick money tempt her, I don't believe that Monica will rejoin the gang. She has eleven grandchildren and wants to spend time with them — to get back the years she feels were wasted with her own four children. Most of her nieces and nephews are hard-core gang members and are in jail. Many nieces work the street for drugs. Monica sees her mission in life as getting these family members out of gang life and staying clean and sober. I think she can do it. Her current girlfriend does not drink or do drugs and has no gang involvement. She is a key support. Monica also has an excellent social worker who has known her for years. Monica says she relies on her to keep on track.

Monica volunteers her time at local schools. She doesn't want a job where she gets paid, as she is afraid that she'll use the money to get a fix. Instead, she survives on her meagre monthly welfare cheques. Although she has taken care of dozens of children and gang members during her adult years, she has only recently come to mother her own children. She still longs for someone who will mother her.

✳ C H A P T E R 4 ✳

I WON'T BACK DOWN

Jake is an imposing figure. Twenty-eight years old, he is six feet two inches tall, weighs 225 pounds, and has blonde hair and blue eyes. He has scars from a stab wound on his chest and bullet wounds in his back and chest. His right hand is deformed from punching people and walls, the pinkie knuckle pushed halfway into the middle of his palm.

He has two full sleeves of tattoos, and many others on his wrists, back, chest, and neck. "They are all related to four things: money, respect, power and women." Those that are gang-related have been partially covered up with new tattoos or simply blackened out. The gang tattoo around his wrist is symbolic of having been shot at and there's another gang tattoo on his chest. The iron cross on his shoulder used to have a swastika in the middle, but that has since been covered. The large tattoo that covers his back and another on his right arm indicate that he is independent and unique, and that he has left gang life. Tattoos of naked women symbolize various aspects of his old life. Finally, a tattoo on his left arm of a person stabbing his own stomach boasts that Jake would die for his personal honour. He has not been hassled by the police, nor by his old associates, since he covered up his gang tattoos.

Jake was adopted at about eight weeks old from a foster home. All he knows about his biological parents, both of whom were Caucasian, is that his mother was a teenager and his father hid the pregnancy from his own parents. To this day he still struggles to understand what makes him tick. "I don't know my genes. After all these years, I lack introspection. The realization that I was different from everyone else didn't happen in my childhood, it only became apparent as I got older and took stock of my life."

Jake's background is somewhat unusual for a gang member. He comes from an affluent family that lives in a middle-class suburb in British Columbia. Both his parents hold good jobs. He has many extended family members and has spent lots of time with them. None of his other family members have ever been involved in gangs or crime. His parents never hid the adoption from him and always told him that they would support him in locating his biological parents if he so desired. "My family life as a child is what I would describe an ideal home. The only piece of the puzzle that didn't seem to fit was me." He never went without — anything he wanted, he got.

Jake's father was very involved in his son's hockey teams. He usually was the coach. His parents' friends were largely made up of other parents who had children on Jake's teams. "We all played on the same hockey teams. We went on vacation together, did pretty much everything together. All things were based around sports with our dads pushing us pretty hard to be the best. We always played on the elite teams that had the best uniforms and went on the biggest tournaments. I loved it." But, even with the enjoyment these activities brought to Jake, he was still different. "If there's one thing that I can say I've loved all my life, it is being elevated in stature over someone in some perceived way, whether real or not. I've always been very good at identifying people's weaknesses and attacking them mercilessly. I've thought many times long and hard about this and still have no answers as to why I was and am like this. I only feel comfortable once I have seemingly subdued everyone around me. I speak very forcefully to this day and still know how to intimidate people in a subtle way through clever speaking." Jake learned much about how to behave from his father, but he also knows that genetic predisposition is important as well. "If it's a learned behaviour, I should be able to let go of it, but I just can't."

Jake's father was a disciplinarian, but he was not abusive either to his wife or son. There was no violence in the home. Jake was yelled at for getting into trouble and occasionally got spanked or "a lighter smack upside the head." Jake believes that he needed physical discipline to deal with his behavioural problems. He reasons that his need for attention and his "wild showmanship streak" were at the root of his problems. He even got kicked out of preschool for being out of control. He enjoyed telling off teachers in front of his peers. His parents were forced to find him a new school when he was only five years old. "I was wildly unpredictable. I would punch another kid in the face just for the sheer fun of it. One time in grade four I took off my belt and tried to whip another kid with it. This behaviour was abhorrent to my parents who tried to discipline me to no avail." Although Jake realizes that his father's parenting strategies were not always the best, he is clear on one issue: he, and he alone, is to blame. "I want this to be my fault, not his. I realize that I am the puppeteer of my own demise, you know?" Jake's father, whom he adores, is his rock and has never abandoned him.

Jake was always obsessed with toughness. He could not retreat once someone started to bother him. His father used to tell him that "it was okay to fight if someone else starts it. [He said] 'Don't let people push you around.' [It's] advice that I still live by to this day." Looking back, Jake wishes that this axiom had never been instilled in him because it has gotten him into so much trouble over the years. He's quick to talk about how much he and his father are alike. They are both explosive. His father has road rage and screams at other drivers, shakes his fist at them, and at times he jumps out of his own car to chase other drivers down. His father never backs down from anyone or anything. Just like Jake.

In grades three and four, Jake's temper got the better of him many times. "I was always a hothead." He was in fights constantly, but he rarely got disciplined. If he said that someone else started it, he would never get in trouble with his father. In fact, his dad never reprimanded him, no matter how violent he was. "It was a Catch-22 for me. All I had to say was that I did not start it. I used to punch people in the face. The school would send a slip home to my parents, but I never got in trouble." Jake hated authority, unless he was the one who was the authoritarian. Even as a youngster, he liked to have power over others. This behaviour "gives me a sense of superiority over others. I have a domineering character. I enjoy besting people."

During his early years, Jake was constantly bored and sought out thrills wherever he could find them. He was diagnosed with Attention Deficit Disorder (ADD) in grade four and was supposed to take Ritalin every day. He hated the drug because it made him feel like a vegetable. "It took the fun out of me and made me a zombie. I was sort of in a catatonic state of paying attention. I lost my need for excitement and it dialled down my aggression; basically, it did everything it was designed to do. I felt like I was so vulnerable when I was taking it; I felt exposed without any of my self-designed armour to protect me." When his mother gave a pill to him before school, he would keep it in his cheek and spit it out into a bush the minute he stepped out of the house. One day, when his father was gardening, he discovered the stash of pills in the bushes. Although Jake laughs now, he got into big time trouble then. Later on, in grade eight, he sold the pills to classmates. He feigned taking Ritalin until grade twelve.

The police started to take note of Jake's behaviour when he

was twelve. He likely would have had more involvement in the justice system earlier on had it not been for Canada's legislation, which stipulates that children under age twelve cannot be held criminally responsible. At age twelve, he was caught stealing clothing from a department store in a mall and was brought home by the cops. This scared him enough to keep him away from any criminal involvement for the next couple of years. But his insatiable appetite for "excitement and high drama" meant that the fighting and bad behaviour continued, although the police never intervened when he was violent at school. Jake had learned to manoeuvre around the law.

Despite problems with aggression and acting out in class, Jake's behaviour in elementary school was a walk in the park compared to his high school experiences. Up until his grade eight graduation, he more or less liked school and found the academic aspect of it easy. He was bright and rarely brought homework home. He was well-liked by fellow students, although many teachers were exasperated by his behaviour. In particular, he drove his grade four teacher nuts. She took stress leave following a particularly nasty sequence of events orchestrated by Jake. "I was constantly pushing her buttons; I hated her. She was very favouring to certain kids and that drove me insane. I decided I would do anything and everything in my power to make her life hell. I would start fights with the kids she favoured, making them afraid to go to her. I would leave class in the middle and disappear, knowing she was responsible for my well-being. And then I would say she yelled at me when the principal would finally find me."

In high school, the fights became more severe. Police were called. As Jake's defiance towards authority increased, his relationship with his parents deteriorated. He provoked and angered his teachers. He first tried smoking pot when he was thirteen and turned to harder drugs in his late teens.

Jake loved money — and what it bought him — and was always scheming to make more. He came up with an ingenious way of milking students at the start of each semester. "I would always collect a bunch of spare locks from Staples, and go around and put them on any available full-size lockers, as they were reserved for the older students. Then I would sell the combinations to the younger students who wanted to be cool and have a big locker like the older kids." Jake sold the locks for twenty dollars each and Ritalin for five dollars a pop. He ran a betting pool on high school football games. He also sold firecrackers. The father of one of his friends was a trucker, and Jake convinced him to bring American firecrackers across the border, which Jake bought from him and then sold for a huge profit at school. He was making as much as one thousand dollars per month. "There is always a demand for something, and I'd always be happy to be the supply." He has no idea why he did these things, apart from his desire for fast cash.

Jake was sixteen when he got himself into trouble by stealing the girlfriend of another student. This resulted in a brawl between his friends, who were white, and a rival group, mainly black, who supported the "lovelorn ex-boyfriend." The black group had a "hate-on" for Jake because he had taunted them with racial slurs the previous day. The fight took place in front of a corner store. Jake repeatedly slammed the ex-boyfriend's head into a large picture window, finally breaking it. "I remember really wanting to hurt this guy, I mean, I literally wanted him dead by my bare hands. I was like a rabid dog. My buddies pulled me off of him." Unfortunately, Jake never suffered any serious consequences. He convinced his father that it was he who was being victimized and that the other group had started the fighting. "I could tell my Dad was proud of me, and it made me feel really great to know that." His father paid for a new window, and the boys had to take part in peer counselling. These were hardly the consequences that would make Jake take responsibility for his violent behaviour. Instead, he grew to understand that he was invincible and above the law.

About the same time, Jake formed a neo-Nazi Skinhead gang with friends he met at summer school. "We basically just all had shaved heads, wore steel-toed boots, drank in parks, and beat people up." They were not into making money. Jake's father was furious because his own father — the grandfather Jake loved so much that later he commemorated his death with a tattoo in his honour — had escaped a Nazi concentration camp during the Second World War. For once, he could not support his son's choices. Although Jake does not like to think of himself now as a perpetrator of racially motivated violence, he always had a "weird fascination" with Nazis. He was attracted to their uniforms, their order and control, and their brutality. He got his first tattoo, a stylized swastika on his shoulder, around the same time he formed this gang.

The gang got drunk and "boot-fucked" people in a local park: they beat up people by kicking them with their steel-toed boots. "All these incidents pretty much happened in the same way. We would see a group of guys, walk up to them and give them one chance to leave our park; if they didn't comply, the fight was on." Once, the Skinheads told a group of East Indian kids to beat it. They didn't, and the fight began. "One guy tried to stab me with a broken bottle, but I moved in time for it to only be a slash." The Skinheads forced the other kids to leave, but about an hour later five carloads showed up. "There was no talking; the fight was on. We held our own considering the ratio was about three to one, but they got the upper hand and beat us pretty senseless." Jake's friends suffered injuries, but nothing too serious. One of Jake's eyes was swollen closed from being repeatedly hit with an axe handle. "It was nothing really of major concern for me."

Jake enjoyed these fights. He had his own code of the street.

He viewed himself as a kind of lone wolf, believing that you should answer to yourself and not to anyone else. "I felt that I was doing my own thinking in my own way." He never carried a gun. It was okay to carry a knife but a sign of weakness to use it. Fighting with fists was the honourable thing to do. He never picked on weaker people.

Jake referred to his fellow members in the Skinheads as "just a bunch of middle-class kids who liked to drink and fight. We hadn't been exposed to any serious criminality or poverty, which makes our behaviour all the more troubling to me." The "browns and whites" were always fighting each other, and the racial divide played out at some schools. Some gangs had mostly East Indian students; others had mostly whites. Jake thrived on the violence and was never affected by being beaten. It didn't matter whether he was the perpetrator or the victim. But the number of beatings he delivered and took did have an impact: he could not feel pain. He had so many concussions that "the room will kind of spin" around him even now when he gets out of bed in the morning.

Jake's involvement with the Skinheads did not last long. After a year or so, he got tired of his parents constantly being on his case. They wanted him to stop his gang involvement. "My Dad hated the Nazis. I felt so ashamed and stupid." He decided to leave the gang. He was not victimized by a brutal beating when he left — the usual punishment meted out — likely because the other members were afraid of him.

Tragedy struck towards the end of this time. One of his best friends was killed during a racially motivated fight between the Skinheads and an East Indian group of students from another school. They came to Jake's school in a large vehicle and shouted racial slurs at the whites. Jake shouted, "There are those Hindus. Let's get 'em." The East Indians took off and were chased down by Jake's group on foot. The car ran into Jake and a friend, who bounced off the hood of the car. But another friend was not as lucky. "I remember all you could hear was the blood-curdling screams of the guy dying. There was a streak of human flesh and blood on the pavement — that image will be with me forever. He was hamburger meat. I mean, I remember we went over there and tried to hold his hand, and he didn't really have a hand."

After this incident, racial tensions were aggravated. Hatred between the two groups broke out in fights everywhere. The police ended up guarding Jake's school to prevent any further attacks. This did little to address the roots of racism, which continued to percolate among his peers.

A year or two after this, Jake graduated from high school and was accepted into college. During his later years in high school, he had taken part in a police-sponsored summer camp, the purpose of which was to learn the basics of law enforcement. He was told that if he completed the course and went on to take college courses in criminology, he would likely be taken on as a new recruit in the force. He enjoyed the camp immensely, particularly the hand-to-hand combat training and techniques used to control suspects. His parents were relieved that he seemed to be on the right track and got off his case.

Jake left college after failing many courses and applied to join the armed forces. He liked taking the medical and psychological exams and loved the concept of being part of a collective that worked like a machine. He had ambitions to become an officer — to have junior people report to him. "It's like it was a group of us against the world type thing." He was fascinated by the weapons and the prospect of bombing the enemy. Then, he was rejected due to his ADD diagnosis. He was crushed. "I was trying to save me from myself. I'm gonna end up fucking dead. I remember being devastated. My self-esteem was at an all-time low. I remember this wave of hopelessness that rushed over me." He no longer had a ticket out of the city he was coming to despise. However, the ever-present schemer in Jake was able to turn this experience into a positive one: the police camp and army training would help him in his criminal career. In fact, "I've impersonated the RCMP many times." This came in handy when Jake was collecting debts from people who owed his gang money. He would knock on their doors pretending to be a police officer and usually gained entry with little resistance. Once inside, Jake would beat them up and collect the money.

So, after a couple of positive years, Jake turned about-face. He now believed that he lived in a dog-eat-dog world and was being punished for trying to turn his life around. Being the "good guy" was not for him: "I simply stopped caring." He spent his time lying around his parents' house, watching crime shows on television and movies such as *Scar Face*. Jake wanted to become a contract killer like Al Pacino's character, making obscene amounts of money; he was not going to flip hamburgers and be under the thumb of an employer.

Jake was eighteen years old. With two of his best friends, he started committing a variety of petty crimes. They broke into homes and stole valuables, damaged property, and picked fights. They developed a scam of stealing license plates, putting them on their own cars, then stealing gas and selling it to people at a reduced price. He was still a wheeler and dealer. His love affair with money was growing and his violence was escalating.

Jake worked at various high-end restaurants during this time, mainly as a cook. He looked for jobs only at places gang members were known to frequent. He took every opportunity to meet older, more hardened gangsters. Most were in their late twenties and early thirties. He partied with them and fought anyone they wanted him to attack. Wearing the wrong hat or looking at someone the wrong way were legitimate reasons to lay a beating on someone. "I had a 'take no prisoners' attitude and I was eager to impress."

Jake was willing to do just about anything to be recognized by the gangsters he was courting. "I was establishing my reputation with the older crowd at the restaurant as someone who was completely off his rocker. We would all go out to bars after work, and I would fight basically on the command of these guys. They really seemed to like that. They would see someone they didn't like and then they would say to me 'we don't like that guy over there, what are you going to do about it?' These guys treated me like a member of the family, a younger brother. So when I perceived any disrespect towards them or anyone we were with, it was my job to clean house." Once, in one bar where they gathered, a man said something to one of the gangster's girlfriends and had even gone into the women's washroom while she was in it. The boyfriend asked Jake to take care of it. "I walked over to the guy who was sitting on a stool and told him that he needed to apologize to the girl. He refused, so I tackled him off the stool and ended up stomping him unconscious." According to Jake, the victim had been given a fair chance to take responsibility for his actions. He didn't. Jake believed he had no other option than to beat him senseless.

Jake's crimes escalated to the point that he committed armed robberies. He lost his childhood friends and became estranged from his family. He glamorized gang life and would do anything to gain the friendship and trust of gangsters. He was both scared and excited by being with them, with the thrills and rush of violence. He partied with biker gangs and made connections with the main dope dealers in the region. He became an enforcer and debt collector for one of the largest and most dangerous gangs in British Columbia.

For a young man who had fought for respect for most of his life, becoming a member of a notorious gang felt like the right thing to do. At twenty years old, he had as many beautiful women as he wanted. He was making $3,000 to $5,000 at a time to beat up rivals. He raked in $15,000 to $20,000 a month for collecting from those who owed money to his gang. When he wasn't ripping off drugs from rival gangs, he would break into their grow-ops, tie up everyone inside and kick and punch them until they were nearly dead. He extorted money from people. He ran dial-a-dope lines where he would send runners out to make his deliveries after users called his drug line, making an order for cocaine or marijuana. He disciplined other gang members. For once in his life, people wanted to be like him. "I was like the boy wonder."

Jake's gang was made up of members from a variety of ethnic and racial groups. Everyone was welcome as long as they could make money, crack skulls, and fly under the radar of the law. Unlike many other gangs in Canada, they did not have to commit survival crimes that were motivated by the need to get housing, food, and other basic necessities of life. Instead, they committed crimes such as debit card fraud, marijuana production and brokering, cocaine sales, and ripping off drug shipments from rivals. Membership had benefits: protection, networking, money, friendship, and a sense of family. "It was more an organization of a bunch of independent drug dealers who banded together for networking and protection. We were more like a union of like-minded dealers. Guys had to respect and listen to their higher-ups but did not have to give money to them." There was a sense of brotherhood in the gang. He was close to certain guys and it was like working in an office. But relationships could get messy: someone could be a friend today, an enemy tomorrow.

Jake was inducted at a dinner and given a gang jacket with his name stitched on it. He was very proud. He liked having a reputation as a badass. "I became a talked-about figure in the circle of people I went to high school with. Everyone wanted to be my friend. At the time I thought it was out of respect, but now looking back I realized that everyone was just afraid of me and didn't want to be on my bad side." Instead of handing over a portion of his profits to higher-ups in the gang, he was expected to help fellow members in their work and give them a good price on drugs. He was not beaten into the gang, nor, later, was he beaten out of it. This is very unusual. Many gangsters have to endure a "blood in, blood out" process.

Although Jake was mostly an enforcer, his preferred work was setting up grow-ops and selling the drugs. He looked upon this as a "long-term investment, which paid constantly." Although he began by ripping off or jacking other people's drug shipments, he came to frown on this activity — it wasn't ethical. Despite belonging to a criminal organization that made huge profits feeding people's addictions, Jake had morals. He began setting up "twenty light" operations: each grow light would yield one pound of weed, and there were twenty lights in each grow house. This made him up to $5,000 every week, and the work was easy and low-risk. He also was running coke and crack distribution lines in parts of the country where rival groups could not challenge his work. Often, other gangs co-operated with Jake and moved the dope for his gang. Toronto was a favourite destination. One pound of marijuana sold for about $3,500 there, whereas where Jake lived it was closer to $2,000.

On one occasion, Jake was running a crack line in town. A buyer took off with drugs without paying. Jake tracked him down to his first-floor apartment and fired warning shots through the ceiling. "It was one of the stupidest things I ever did. Of course the people in the apartment on the second floor would notice." Jake recovered his money and beat the guy to within an inch of his life. Dressed in his gang attire, Jake terrified the neighbours, who quickly got out of his way. He did the job in plain daylight and was not apprehended by the police.

Media outlets often report on gangs being at war with each other. For the most part, this was not the case for Jake's gang. There were more conflicts within the gang than there were with rival groups. The goal was to make as much money as possible through drug trafficking and rip-offs (stealing large quantities of drugs from rival gangs). If that could be done in collaboration with another gang, so be it. Internal tensions grew out of personal beefs. For example, if one member was thought to have disrespected a higher-up by coming on to his girlfriend, he was beaten to a pulp and kicked out of the gang. It didn't matter if the story was true or not. It was all about perception.

Jake's gang was at war, though, with another high-profile gang in the province. They hated each other and fought constantly for control over turf. The rival gang was family-based and had been formed in a young offender centre among high school friends. It terrorized the province, killing suspected enemies and innocent people in broad daylight. "This gang told us 'we want your customers. I dare you to say no.'" For the most part, Jake's gang was able to stay out of their way, but vicious fights between them were not uncommon.

Towards the end of Jake's gang life, he became a freelancer — or "crew jumper" — with the tacit approval of other members who didn't cause him any problems. People who had money owing them contracted him to collect. A gang member would give Jake details of the case — who the debtor was, how much he owed, his last known address and telephone number, and contact information on family members. Jake negotiated a price and received a down payment. He then would "skulk around the place, try to find phone bills, or intimidate people who were there into telling me where [the debtor] was." Some jobs were easier than others. At times the target was in town and could be found within a couple of days. Others had gone into hiding and had to be chased across the country. "On collections where people would leave the province, I would always start with their phone bills, then reverse lookup the numbers they were calling. And if those numbers were all in Ontario or Quebec or pretty much anywhere, I'd just get on a plane and go." A typical case involved a $5,000 up-front payment. Then, Jake would gather his information and take off on a two-week romp across the country looking for the target. Upon completion of the job, he was paid the remainder of the contract — usually another $5,000 to $10,000. The most money he ever collected on a debt was $170,000. He was paid 10 per cent for that job — $17,000.

Jake was frequently a victim as well as a perpetrator of violence. He was stabbed, run over, beat up, shot at, and extorted by rivals. His parents were threatened. "Looking back on it, it was awful." He was loyal and had no fear. "I was like a dog." He began to carry a handgun constantly. "I got progressively stupider every time I drank," he says. "I had a gun in a strip club. I was searched by the cops, but a girl was holding it in her purse. At one point I asked her to pass it to me and the cops arrested me."

Jake was doing a lot of cocaine, although he did not see himself as an addict. "I was a mess. I was always bored and had nothing to do." He built up a tremendous tolerance to it and snorted huge amounts of the drug. Buying cocaine was not a problem. He would make a couple thousand dollars for settling a score one day and then partied for the rest of the night and most of the next day. He usually did this in clubs with other gangsters. "I just liked doing it and there was nothing else to do." Because of his expensive habit, he usually ended up owing someone money. "There was no such thing as easy money. The money always had karma attached. You'd end up losing somehow and you'd owe so and so for this. Or this guy would take off with your stuff; it was stressful." One night, Jake paid nine hundred dollars for some coke he bought in a club. The police were all over the place. Jake was in need of a rush to offset his boredom. So he left the club, got in his car, and drove around "like a lunatic," hoping he'd be stopped by a cruiser so he could pick a fight with the officers: "I could have gone nuts with them." For whatever reason, the police never caught up with him that night.

When Jake turned twenty-five, he began to think about his future. He was tired of looking over his shoulder. Friends were getting killed, becoming addicts, or just went missing. His family hated him. The Russian mob tried to kill him for losing a $30,000 drug shipment to the police. The Russians, ex-Red Army types, had grow-ops but lacked the manpower to chop the weed, dry it, and pack it. Jake ran "cutting crews," some of whom were prostitutes known to his gang. "I had a load of their stuff and stashed it. I had sixty pounds and the cops took it." This was not the first time the cops had come after Jake. But it was the first time that he was stashing a crop for another criminal organization and it was confiscated and destroyed.

The police were alerted to the grow-op because the guy Jake put in charge of renting the house missed his rent payment. Instead he blew the money on drugs. The landlord, who had no idea what the house was being used for, showed up and saw a heap of firearms on a table. He called the police. Jake was furious because he had invested "a shitload" of money into the oper-ation; now, he had to figure out a way to repay the mob. He did so with drugs and cash that he borrowed from friends. He then had to pay his friends back.

By this time, Jake was constantly being arrested. He was con-victed of a variety of offences, including gun and drug crimes, and was sent to jail. He shared a cell with the leader of another notorious gang that sold cocaine and was the biggest criminal organization in the province. "This gang made us look like Mr. Rogers." According to Jake, jail was a "real *Lord of the Flies*-type setting." It was violent, boring, putrid, and loud. Riots broke out from time to time. He stayed drunk or high on drugs. "The worst part for me was that I now had to live alongside all the junkies and addicts I'd helped create. These peoples' lives were ruined due to my actions. No drug dealer ever stops and thinks about the lives he destroys, but I did." Jake was lonely in jail. His mother never came to see him, although his father and younger brother visited periodically. He had time to think about what he had become. He was ashamed about the harm he had brought to his family. He wanted to mend fences.

When he was released from jail, Jake got a traditional job as a mechanic and felt normal making money from a legitimate business. He was enjoying life. But he felt indebted to his cellmate, and the allure of drugs and easy money kept pulling him back into the gang. He brokered drug deals at night after work, drank in bars, and fought. He was moving twenty pounds of marijuana at a time and making up to $4,000 per job. "I was still dabbling in the drug world but had basically told everyone, 'Don't expect much from me — I'm burnt out.'" He decided he had done all he needed to pay his obligation to the leader of the other gang. Then he met Nicki, and everything changed. Love of this woman gave him the courage to leave the gang for good.

Although Jake had all the women he wanted while in the gang, Nicki is different. She is intelligent, educated, and has a good job. Jake tells her everything and she listens. She doesn't judge him but helps him reflect on the negative aspects of his life. She makes him believe that he is worth something and has unlimited potential. This is not new for Jake. Loving family members have been telling him this most of his life. It's different this time. "She saved my life." They're getting married next year.

Leaving the gang has not been as hard as Jake expected. "I said goodbye to the drug scene and got rid of all my BlackBerries, contacts, and told everyone I no longer wanted to be involved. This was met with a collective yawn from a group of people who claimed to be my family and brothers for so many years." Jake still clings to some reminders: he keeps his gang attire and gang-related photos at his parents' house, in the closet of his old room.

Jake takes pride in the fact that he has no enemies. He believes he always "played the game straight," at least after he stopped ripping off the drug shipments and grow-ops of rivals. He left the gang without a moment to spare. A good friend who remained was beaten so badly that he is now brain damaged and in a wheelchair for the rest of his life. Jake has to constantly remind himself that he just has too much to lose if he were to live the way he used to, allowing his anger to boil over into violence. "I was at Tim's [Tim Hortons coffee shop] the other day. A chick screwed up on my order. It just drove me absolutely nuts. It bugs me, but I won't say anything. Inside, I'm angry." Another night, Jake and Nicki went to the movies. The people behind them kept talking. "I just wanted to turn around and strangle them! Ha ha, but I can't do that anymore, right?"

He still has problems with impulse control. When he sees a commercial on television for a fast food restaurant, he will jump in his car and go get a burger, even if he's just eaten dinner. He can't resist the urge. "It's like I'm a slave to my whims." It's not just about hamburgers, though, it's also about being a slave to his feelings of not backing down. "If I leave a situation where I feel like someone has punked me out or disrespected me, like, it will just gnaw at me. I lose my temper quite quickly and am sometimes extremely paranoid about things for no reason. I sometimes regret the way I act with people later."

Jake has another side to him. He can be very compassionate and will give the shirt off his back to someone in need. For people he believes deserve to be helped, he is the first one there to lend a hand. But he has no time for losers. One of his mottos is: "treat me good, I'll treat you better. Treat me bad, I'll treat you worse."

Jake is no longer on parole. He works as a heavy machine mechanic four days a week. He is also in his second year of university, studying psychology, and he is working on a community gang prevention project. Jake calls his past life "hell." Money is tight these days, but he doesn't miss the drugs and huge profits. "People ask me if I miss it and I can honestly say that some parts I do, but the pain and misery you inflict on yourself and the world around you just isn't worth it."

Jake considers himself to be one of the lucky ones. Not only did he make it out of the gang alive, but he is also enjoying life with all of its day-to-day challenges. He has come to value and appreciate his family. Although he still does not understand what about himself led to life in the gang, he desperately wants to find answers — not only to help in his own healing journey, but also to help prevent other young people from becoming involved in the life. "Just like my Dad used to tell me. Don't back down. That got me into lots of trouble in my younger years. But now it means something completely different."

✳ CHAPTER 5 ✳

WHAT A RUSH IT WAS

Janie, aged twenty-six, is a strikingly beautiful young woman. At five feet five inches, she is solidly built and has shoulder-length brown hair. She is soft-spoken and giggles when she talks. She wears a blue hoodie and blue sweatpants. She's covered in tattoos. On her right shin is a covered-up tattoo representing the rape she experienced when she was young; she doesn't want to be reminded of that anymore. On her right calf are three monkeys representing her three eldest children. On the same leg is a Winnie the Pooh tattoo for herself. On her left calf, a flower obliterates an old gang tattoo. There's also a rather obscure homemade tattoo on the same leg. Janie put it on herself when she was ten. "It's supposed to be my name, but I did a bad job." A dolphin on her right shoulder and a flower on her left shoulder cover up gang tattoos. When she was a teen, her mother gave her a tattoo of a dreamcatcher on her left wrist. A large tattoo on her back bears the name "George." It is to be blackened over next month.

Janie was born into a gang family. Her father was never in the picture since he had a one-night stand with her mother and never came back. Until this day she mourns the loss of not having a father figure. She desperately wanted a dad when she was a child. Yet, Janie remembers a happy early childhood. "I loved my life at first. It was me and my mom. No one else."

That changed when her brother, Tom, was born. Janie was four years old and jealous; she bullied him incessantly. Once, she pushed her little brother down the stairs in his walker. Another time, when he was in his stroller, she pushed him off the porch. She was mean to him only when she was left alone to look after him. "I beat on him when Mom was not at home. I threw things at him, like full tobacco cans." She punched and hit him. She would also dare him to do dangerous tricks. She persuaded him to do a front flip, which he didn't know how to do. He landed on his face and "launched his nose into his brain."

Janie did well in school at first. Her mother was just dabbling in gang life at the time and her drug use was more or less under control. Janie liked her kindergarten teacher, who was a lot of fun. But that same year she bit a kid's nose so hard that she broke it. "He was just bugging me. He got on my nerves." Janie's mother took her out of school for a month, and the victim transferred out. Janie returned to the same school but never got picked on for hurting that little boy. Janie's mother was afraid that Janie would hurt other kids, but Janie was the one who was bullied until she figured out that she could take on most kids and win. "I was just a mean kid."

Like her mother, Janie was sexually abused at a young age. An uncle forced himself on her from the time she was five years old. The sexual abuse was particularly devastating for Janie. The uncle gave her sleeping pills about half an hour before the abuse occurred to make it easier for him to do whatever he wanted. He sent her sexually explicit letters in which he threatened her to keep her mouth shut.

She began cutting herself, without wanting to kill herself,

at age nine. This is common for girls who are surviving sexual abuse. "I felt better when I cut; it was good to see the blood. I felt alive." Her wrists and forearms are covered in small, thin cuts in straight, parallel lines that look like railroad tracks — there are too many scars to count.

Janie was nine and George was seventeen when they became friends; they spent their time drinking, drugging, and socializing with other gang members. Her mother and George's mother were good friends (and still are) and Janie's mother was a higher-up in the gang of which George was one of the leaders. George had been hanging out with gangsters while Janie was still in diapers.

Janie found him cool and fun to be around. He would say to her, "Be down and always be protected." She spent much of her childhood with friends that were nine and ten years older than her because she thought kids her own age were "too immature." She followed the "in-crowd" into gang life because she wanted to be included and not left out. And she liked the drugs and alcohol. "I thought I was living a really cool life."

The uncle who was abusing her also made nude videos and pictures of Janie and some of her friends, and sent them over the Internet to family and other friends. It is unclear if he ever sold them. Her family turned on her because they thought Janie was the one taking the pictures and sending them out for attention, although she was only eleven. Some of her best friends told their parents. The parents also assumed that it was Janie who was taking the pictures and ordered their kids not to play with her any more. Janie told her mother about the abuse at this time. Her mother immediately understood Janie's pain because she herself had been abused as a child for many years. Janie had been reluctant to tell her mother before this time due to the threats made by her abuser. With her mother's support, she gave a statement to the police and her uncle was charged with multiple counts of sexual assault and convicted. He faced more charges in another province for sexually assaulting other young girls and was convicted there as well. When Janie told her mother about the abuse, she was able to prove it by the letters that she'd kept. She gave them all to her mother.

In about grade four or five, as her rage was building, she turned into a bully, though she still needed protection from others in her school who were as angry and aggressive as she was.

Her attendance at school was good when she was around, but she missed a lot of school when she stayed at her aunt's house. Her mom was heavily gang-involved by this point and was also taking care of Janie's aunt, who was very sick. It was a four-hour trip from Janie's house to where her aunt was staying (Janie's mom took her along on these trips), so she often didn't make it back in time for school or was too tired to go. She had a short attention span. She got bored easily, daydreaming and wanting to be outside.

A couple of months after she told her mother about the sexual abuse, and despite her mother's support at that time, Janie felt her family had rejected and abandoned her. She thought about her father: "maybe he doesn't want me in his life." Her mother was often too stoned to take care of her, or was out dealing drugs. She started to run away from home. "I didn't listen to my mom. I knew that she was a gang member and addict, and that she didn't want this lifestyle for me. But I chose it anyway." She was often apprehended by child welfare and spent time in many foster homes.

The fighting at school finally stopped and her grades were good in grade six. She played forward on the school soccer team and scored many goals.

Grade seven was a different story. Janie started smoking weed. By the age of twelve she was popping sleeping pills, Gravol, and anything else she could find that would get her high. She stole sleeping pills from family members and bought or stole Gravol, taking dozens of pills at once. The high lasted for about eight hours and much longer if she smoked weed at the same time. "It was like being on acid with lots of hallucinations. It was a good high." She bought the Gravol in bottles of 100 pills and persuaded friends to buy her more when she ran out. She built up a tremendous resistance to the pills and was taking handfuls at a time.

At school she fought often, got many detentions, attended sporadically, and was suspended frequently. Other kids made fun of her family because they were involved with gangs and were very poor. Janie prided herself in not throwing the first punch. She reasoned that she could not be charged with assault if she used violence in self-defence. "I pushed them up against the wall, but I let them hit me first. If they got me in the face, I'd black out. Then I would knock them out." Janie dropped out in grade seven, halfway through the school year. She was thirteen years old.

Janie officially joined the gang when she dropped out of school. Her mother had been a member for many years, and George had been a vice-president for the past eight years. Along with two other founding members, he had patched over from a more established gang to the new gang. He took the top job when the previous president was sentenced to life for murdering a rival.

George used to dress all in blue — jeans, shoes, socks, shirt, jacket, even his underwear — and the police could spot him a mile away just by the colour of his clothes. Janie was a particularly attractive recruit to the gang leaders because she had no criminal record. Her lack of involvement in the justice system had nothing to do with her actual behaviour. In fact, she committed many serious crimes. She was just good at hiding out from the cops.

Janie was beaten into the gang. At George's direction, two women — his sister and an ex-girlfriend — punched and kicked her for a set number of minutes, but Janie was not allowed to fight back. "I was pretty beat up. I took my minutes and I was down." Janie had seen this ritual many times before and knew it was coming. Although her mother supported the beating-in process for new recruits, she didn't want her daughter to go through this ordeal. But George was the higher-up and he overruled Janie's mother. Even though he was close friends with Janie, he insisted that she take her minutes.

Janie was a striker at first. She got orders to do home invasions and robberies. "To me it was just fun and games." Then she moved up to be a drug runner. This was a more prestigious position because she had to hold thousands of dollars and be trusted to turn it over to her higher-ups. She handed off wads of money to get kilos of cocaine, which she brought back to the leaders. Other members would cut it up, mix it with protein powder, bag it, and then give it to low-level members to sell on the street. Janie also took orders from George to protect the status of male gang members. Her job was to beat up girls who bad-mouthed them. "I laid a lickin' on them for George."

Because of the sexual abuse, among other things, Janie tried to kill herself three times during her adolescence by slitting her wrists. She never had any therapy or other supports to help her deal with the trauma. She felt isolated and alone, despite being a part of the gang. She continued to blame herself for the abuse and developed a hatred for herself. "The abuse made me feel depressed for a while, that I was a nobody and I was not meant to be here. I thought everyone was against me." As well, she was in the company of older men in the gang, and although they never sexually assaulted her, she felt that they saw her as little more than a sexual object. She told me that these men stared at her body parts often and made jokes about how they would like to get into her pants.

When her mother caught her cutting, she took Janie to a doctor who prescribed Paxil, a medication for depression and anxiety. She was in her early teens and hated the way the drug made her feel. She often stopped taking it for weeks at a time, and then started again. Neither she nor her mother knew that this drug is contraindicated for teens: sudden stopping and starting can actually make a person more suicidal. The doctor never explained this. Due to changes in Janie's behaviour, her mother took her off the drug when Janie was about fourteen.

Continually craving a better high, she started using powder cocaine at age fourteen and then crack by the time she was fifteen. She never had to pay for the coke because by then she was working hard for the gang. Many times, instead of being paid in cash for her work, she chose drugs. She smoked crack and drank just about every day. Janie started snorting morphine about the same time.

She was never involved in selling drugs to customers on the street. She was good with money and was trusted to take care of the gang's finances. She also had status because she was such good friends with the vice-president, George. Although he brutalized her, she also benefitted from his position in the gang, whose members feared him enough not to beat on her. He also protected her from working in the sex trade. Although he pestered her constantly about this, Janie stood her ground and refused to work the stroll. This was one of the few decisions she made that he respected.

Due to her money management skills and her relationship with George, Janie rose up the hierarchy. At the time, she and George were friends and gang associates. "Then I became leader of the women. What a rush it was. I got respect." She was sending out orders and directing hits on people. She was telling women what to do, no matter what their age. She particularly liked being the boss of women in their late twenties and thirties when she was not even eighteen years old. And she could take out whomever she wanted. It did not matter if her opponent could win the fight — Janie was always allowed to win because she was top dog. Not only was she the president of the women's auxiliary, she was also the treasurer for both the women's and men's gangs. George's ex-sister-in-law was the vice-president of the women's auxiliary. This caused considerable tension between Janie and George because Janie didn't like the woman. "She was way older and it felt good and powerful to be her higher-up. To know that she hated me for that and that she couldn't do nothing made me in control." Under the vice-president was the general, Liz, who was Janie's best friend. Under the general were dozens of strikers who carried out orders as directed.

Being the president of the women, Janie was responsible for establishing a code of conduct for gang members. "Guys could only use body shots on girls, like punches to the torso, but only if I ordered it. Head shots were only allowed in guys against guys or girls against girls fights. Coming onto the boyfriends of girls was strictly against my rules, same as ripping off members of your own gang." Finally, hard drug abuse was not permitted initially. But, due to Janie and George's addictions, higher-ups in the gang were allowed to use chemicals, as long as they were stable enough to direct gang activity.

People noticed a change in Janie. She became aggressive, violent, and addicted to money. She was also addicted to drugs. Janie told me that her power made her feel drunk. Some days she would pocket $8,000 from trafficking cocaine. By the time Janie was twenty years old, she had two daughters whose fathers were not in the picture. Child welfare took her children away for one year because of her involvement with the gang and the family's living conditions. Her drug use escalated and she didn't care about looking after herself or anyone else. Looking back now, she believes she was a monster.

Janie became very drunk at her own birthday party. She and George had sex. "Then it just happened. I never was attracted to him before that. I always knew that there was something wrong going on. It just happened. I was in too deep." After they were married, his true nature came out. He started slapping and punching her. That went on for about a month. Then he began to beat her routinely and viciously. He cracked her ribs, punched her in the face, and split her lips. Her family, and his, saw the abuse but did nothing. Her mother-in-law told her that she was to blame.

Shortly into their marriage, when she was carrying his twins, George beat her until she was unconscious. She lost one of the babies and the other one, her son, suffered serious injuries in the womb.

When her son was born, George seemed to be an okay father. This was short-lived. He drank from the minute he woke up until he passed out at night. He partied with his soldiers and runners in the gang. He treated his son better than Janie's other kids and was violent with everyone but the boy. "I was scared of him. He was beating me like I was another guy. He didn't care." Their friends and Janie's family tried to get him to stop, but it made no difference. His own mother was afraid of him. The fact that he was the only boy in his family didn't help. He was afraid to be seen as a "mommy's boy."

Janie learned that George had been smoking crack and injecting cocaine for many years before they got married. "He was good at keeping things secret. Part of me knew something was wrong." He tried to kill her once when he was high. He held her down and started strangling her. Her eldest daughter was watching. Luckily her brother, Tom, was visiting at the time and managed to pull George off and beat him up. Strung out on drugs and alcohol, George didn't put up much of a fight. Janie was on her way to having all of her children removed by child welfare, in large part because she was unable to protect them from George's violence and because of their involvement in gang life.

Janie was president for three years. Her underlings called her "Queen." To this day, she takes great pride in being known as the Queen because of the respect it afforded her, both then and now. "It was a whole different experience, sending out orders and hits on people. The power gave me a rush, the same as coke did for me." Although she liked the authority that came with the position, she always looked over her shoulder for George. She understood that her position was solely due to George being president of the men. "He told me that was my role in gang life. I did what he would say. I did not want to argue. I was really scared of him."

With both Janie and George in charge, mistakes and mis-understandings began to get in the way of business. Although he gave her the marching orders, sometimes they had power struggles. Janie liked coming up with her own ideas instead of waiting for George to tell her what to do. She considered it as a form of payback for the wicked beatings he laid on her. So, behind his back, she started to give direction to male soldiers to whom he also was giving direction. Orders got mixed up. Money was lost. When someone had to be disciplined for ripping off the gang, Janie would send soldiers to do the beating. George would send his own soldiers to beat the same guy. Debt collectors were sent by both Janie and George to collect from the same person. Chaos resulted. This only served to fuel George's violence against Janie.

Janie drove out the other street gangs from the city core. She gave the independent drug dealers three choices: they could get beaten into her gang, pay a weekly tax (usually $500) to her and continue to operate, or she would order a hit on their lives. Her underlings were making fistfuls of money selling points and eight balls (3.5 grams of cocaine). But she became careless. She was strung out all the time. George accused her of ripping money off him. He continued to beat her. A prostitute went to the police with information on the gang. The cops rushed their house and Janie and many other members were busted for trafficking cocaine. She got convicted and ended up serving six months, with an additional twelve months probation.

Usually, Janie was good at evading the police and rival gangs. She always wore a blue bandana covering her face so that her rivals rarely knew who was attacking them. "I always made sure I was not noticed."

Janie needed a truck to facilitate the movement of drugs in her trafficking network. Her mother was now an intravenous coke addict so Janie bribed her with points to get the use of her truck. She went on drug runs to other cities, buying large quantities of ecstasy, weed, and coke. She supervised the filling of points with cocaine: straws and small spoons were used to fill each needle "up to the 10 line." The points were given to her runners to sell on the street. When a runner had $1,000 from sales, typically after a three-day period, she would collect the money and provide the runner with more points to sell. She rented hotel rooms in which she waited for her runners to complete the transactions. Her mark-up was usually 300 per cent: if she paid $1,000 to her distributor, she would make $3,000 on the street for selling the same quantity.

A young woman who was not affiliated with any gang ripped one of Janie's drug runners off. In retaliation, Janie and the gang beat her up in front of her children, who saw everything. Janie broke her jaw and ribs. Terrified that Janie would come after her kids if she ratted, the woman didn't go to the police. When she started fighting, Janie would get so angry that, just like when she was in school, she would black out and go so completely out of control that other gang members would have to drag her away to stop her from going too far. "I don't stop until I see lots of blood and they don't move any more. I know they're hurt bad enough then."

One year into their marriage (which lasted three years), when George was twenty-nine years old, he had a sexual relationship with a thirteen-year-old girl — a member of Janie's extended family whom she considered to be a close friend, a younger sister. Janie found out. She blames and hates the girl for what happened, but she could do nothing about it. She thought George would kill her if she told.

Janie is still trying to understand why her husband had sex with young girls — she knows there was more than one and that the abuse went on for years. "I think he was nuts." She can comprehend his behaviour only by seeing it as a problem in his brain.

It's ironic: as boss, he ordered his own soldiers not to sleep with underaged girls. "He gave his boys shit. He said 'I don't want to see you being hounds [pedophiles].' And he was the biggest hound of them all." When some of his underlings in the gang found out about the relationship with the girl, they confronted him. Because he's their boss, they have agreed not to tell anyone. If they do, he will order their deaths.

When Janie confronted George about the affair, his violence escalated. Janie escaped being beaten to death because someone else became his victim first.

As George and Janie spiralled deeper and deeper into using drugs and as they were brawling not only with each other but also with rival gang members, the situation in their house grew more and more tense. One night, when they were there alone, Janie was wakened by the sounds of an argument and fist fighting. She crept downstairs to see George drag a semi-conscious man into the kitchen, where he bound him to a chair with strips of duct tape. She recognized a member of a rival gang who had been poaching on their territory and whom George had invited to come and talk matters over with. George picked up a knife and repeatedly stabbed the guy who screamed and cried out for mercy. Janie rushed forward to stop the torture but George backhanded her so hard she fell to the floor. He plunged the knife into his victim's stomach. "I saw him take his last breath. He was all stabbed up and blood was everywhere."

When George stumbled into the living room, she heard him preparing a fix. She followed him and told him that she wanted out and was calling the police. "It was an experience that made me open my eyes. It still bothers me to know innocent life was taken." Right then and there, she decided that she had to get out. What kind of life would her kids have if she continued in this lifestyle? But George threatened her against leaving, saying "We're bound through marriage by blood and God." Janie called the police a couple of hours after having words with George. They arrived immediately. Janie was arrested, and it took the police until the next day to find George.

At the trial, Janie didn't have to testify against George because they were married at the time. But, knowing what she knew about the crime, he ordered a hit on her. He wanted her killed by some of his underlings. A group of inmates beat her to a pulp. It was then that Janie realized that he didn't care for her. Ordering her to be killed was different from all the times he beat her. He had never involved anyone else in harming her, apart from when she got beaten into the gang. Although family members knew about his violence against Janie, it was still relatively hidden from most people. Ordering the hit, however, was a public display of his vengeance.

George did not admit that he was the murder's sole perpetrator. He never told police that Janie was innocent of the murder but let her hang in the wind, hoping that she would admit to the crime and do the time for him. Janie spent two years in prison before she was proven innocent. Child welfare took her children — three daughters, aged nine, seven, and two, and her four-year-old son — for the two years she was inside.

Witnessing this murder affected Janie profoundly and now she believes that it opened the door for her to exit gang life. George will be in prison for life.

✳ ✳ ✳

Janie has been out of prison for eighteen months and she lives in a house with five other adults and six children (all extended family members and friends) until she finds her own apartment. She recently got the two older girls back and has just given birth to another girl. She's confident the other two children will be returned when she finds a better place in which to live. Last year, at the age of twenty-four, she beat her crack addiction. She's very concerned for her kids: she believes that George will send out some of his subordinates to have them kidnapped and harmed. She divorced him a couple of months ago.

Junior, her boyfriend of the past three years, is the father of her new baby, as well as of her two-year-old daughter. He's an ex-member of the gang, but exited two years ago, wanting no association with a gang that harbours a man like George.

The house is clean, but cluttered. The kitchen table is covered with baby supplies: disposable diapers, bottles of formula, blankets, a plastic bathtub, diaper rash cream, and baby bottles with pictures of Tigger and Eeyore on them.

Since getting out of prison, Janie has gone back to school and will soon receive her high school diploma. She loves social studies but despises math, even though she was so good at managing money in the gang. "In the gang, it's like I had a job in business administration. I was an accountant, really. I was fine with all that money in front of me. But a page full of math is confusing." She wonders if she has some kind of learning disability since her mother abused drugs and alcohol during her pregnancy. Her own son is slow to walk and his speech is delayed due to George's violence towards Janie when she was pregnant with the twins.

George is very possessive and goes into a jealous rage if he thinks Janie is messing with another man. Even though they are no longer together, he tries to control who she is with. He has put a death wish out on Junior. Now, from behind bars, George has threatened to kill Janie if she doesn't go back to leading the female auxiliary of his gang, one of the most dangerous in Western Canada. He has sent his captains and vice-president to threaten her.

Janie says that one of the reasons George so badly wants her back in the gang is because "I have lots of stuff on him that no one knows." She has intimate knowledge of his crimes, some of which are very serious. "He's beaten me so bad and tried to kill me. The trouble I could cause if I testified against him!" The police don't know that he's the perpetrator of these and other crimes. She also knows who George has screwed over and to whom he owes money. George could take lots of heat if the word gets out. Since he's been in prison, the gang has spiralled into chaos and internal violence. He's fighting to maintain his leadership even though he is sitting in a prison cell.

To this day George fears that the secret of his affairs with the underage girls will get out to other inmates who are in rival gangs. As a pedophile, he would be labeled a "skinner" or "hound" and would be subject to all kinds of abuse. He now spends most of his time in protective custody and recently tried to patch over to a new prison gang, thinking that it might give him more protection inside. It's one of the reasons he wants to have Janie killed: to keep her from telling.

Before being sent to prison, George looked like a hyperactive pit bull: just an inch taller than Janie, he weighed about 180 pounds. He wore his hair in a long Mohawk that extended two feet down his back. Even when he was sitting, he fidgeted constantly, his feet so restless that his knees would drum against the tabletop.

Since going to prison, he's shaved off the long hair and gained a lot of weight. He tries to hide his flab by puffing out his chest and strutting around, but he doesn't fool many inmates. Even on the streets, he wasn't as tough as he still pretends to be.

Janie would like to open a store for Aboriginal families, selling food and clothes at cheap prices. "I want to be there to help people." She's also thinking of a career in child and youth care. Young mothers seeking advice on parenting, school, addictions, and gangs often approach her. "They've heard of me!" She helped set up a school program where young, at-risk mothers can bring their babies to class. One told Janie that she was on the verge of losing her kids to child welfare due to her addictions. When Janie helped her out, she said, "I have a lot to thank you for."

Many of the same teachers Janie tormented before she left school are now the teachers of her children. She is determined that her kids will complete high school. She doesn't want them to drop out like she did. These teachers seem to be going the extra mile for her kids, and she often seeks guidance from them.

Janie's family has been very supportive of her exit from gang life. They had been on her case for years to stop the drugs and get rid of George. The pressure was constant from her mom, brother, aunts, and uncles. "They told me, 'It's about time you got out; you don't need that life.'"

Child welfare is involved in Janie's life, but she doesn't mind. It's nothing new to her. She spent considerable time in foster homes as a child, as did her mother. Her grandparents were in a residential school. Janie was in so many different homes that she doesn't remember what any of the places looked like. Neither is she able to describe her many foster parents. It's all a blur: she was so high and drunk for much of that time that her memory is shaky. Her own kids have also spent a lot of time in foster homes, most recently while she was in jail.

Janie likes her child welfare social worker who is very supportive but blunt as a hammer. In her late thirties, the social worker has four kids of her own and knows what it's like to be a parent. She's been working with Janie to get her two younger children back from foster care. Janie has done everything asked of her. She got out of the gang and took parenting classes. She quit drugs and alcohol and participated in a sexual abuse survivors group. She's getting her own apartment. With the social worker's help, "I've come a long way."

For many years, another youth worker has supported Janie. "She told me, 'Get out of that gang life, quit the drugs, be a mom to those kids.'" It took Janie a couple of years to heed this advice. Her own mother was in the gang and addicted for twenty-five years; Janie was in the gang for only ten years, although she was an addict for all that time. "I guess I was like my mom with the drugs and also my kids taken away. But I hated her at the time and here I am the same."

Janie did well in a court-ordered parenting course. She was only sixteen years old when her first child was born and was worried that she'd lose her to child welfare. "I didn't know much about it. Didn't know about discipline, and how to cope if the kids were up to no good. I was really frustrated all the time." When she got pregnant with her fifth child, her social worker told her that if she stayed clear of alcohol and drugs, and consented to drug testing every two weeks, there was no need to worry that the baby would be taken.

Life for Janie is still challenging. Money is tight and she misses the quick cash that came from selling drugs. She figures that she must have made about $100,000 profit from her work in the gang. She was socking it away for when she would get her children back. George took it all. When they were together, George even made her sign over her family allowance cheques to him.

Janie has flashbacks to the sexual abuse and the murder. She has learned to avoid movies about gangsters and crime, which bring back memories too vivid to bear. She keeps herself occupied to ward off these bad thoughts. Having the baby and the other kids with her helps: she's too busy and has less time to think about her uncle and George. Sometimes, Junior finds that she has a "blank look and stares off into space." Such dissociation is a common coping mechanism for survivors of traumatic events.

Not long ago, some members of a rival gang came after Janie to give her a beating because they had a beef with George inside the prison and believed that she was still married to him. When she explained her situation — that she had left the gang and was divorced from George — they became friends. They protect her from past enemies that are still involved in gang life.

Janie seems to be doing all the right things to stabilize her life and become a better parent. She is clean, out of the gang, has complied with court-ordered treatment, and is securing appropriate housing. I believe that she genuinely wants to maintain these positive changes. She was very forthright with me in the interviews and was insightful about her life and future. But, she still faces many risks. She still associates with gang members, has been off drugs for not very long, and has only begun to deal with the sexual trauma she experienced as a youngster.

Janie's eldest child started running away to friends' places when she was five years old. Now nine, when she runs, Janie doesn't know where she goes. The daughter has identified her father, who is in prison, and wants to visit him there. There's no way Janie will let this happen. Janie can't help but see the parallels with her own childhood: her daughter wants to have her father in her life. Janie fears that she may be the evil queen whose mirrored image will tear apart her family.

CHAPTER 6

I'VE GOT TO THROW OUT THE BONES NOW

Dillon, aged thirty-three, is a Latino man, five feet eight inches tall, weighing about 180 pounds. He has a thick frame and likes to cross his arms, revealing his large biceps and shoulders. The pink shirts he often wears are disarming. His hair is black and short and so slicked back with gel that he looks like he just got out of the shower. He wears a silver watch on his left wrist and a silver bracelet on his right, a leather necklace with a white pendant made of bone around his neck, and diamond studs in both ears. He has five tattoos: a gothic cross on his left forearm, the names of his two kids on each arm, the initials of his ex-wife on the back of his neck, and an old gang tattoo that has been covered over with a painting by one of his family members who is a well-known artist.

Dillon struggles to rid his words of street slang. He often mixes Spanish with English. His favourite sayings are "Tonce que?" (What's good?) and "Cuals el pedo?" (What's your beef?). He considers himself to be "the smart one." He lives in a small three-bedroom apartment in a three-story building in one of the largest urban centres in the country. He plays in a jazz band at night and is a manager at a national clothing chain store by day. He is divorced and has two teenaged children.

Dillon's life has been marked by upheaval. He was born in Canada, but his family moved to a South American country where they lived from the time he was eight until he was thirteen. He had a hard time adjusting. He didn't speak Spanish when the family moved south. Then, when they moved back to Canada, his English was poor. He was very lonely and isolated because of his language deficits.

Both Dillon's parents were professionals, but his mother, a teacher, stayed at home after the birth of his sister who is five years his senior. He also has a brother who is two years older than he is. Their father had a good job with an international company, but he was always working, most often away from home. All Dillon wanted was to have a dad who would play sports with him and take him out. Instead, when he was home, his father was distant and cold. His brother was his best friend, and they were inseparable as children. His sister was like a mother to him, and they remain close.

The family was, and still is, very religious. Dillon's father, who is highly respected in the Latino communities both in Canada and his country of origin, is a pastor and, according to Dillon, has a "doctor in theology of the Bible." His mother and brother are pastors as well, although on a part-time basis. His sister is a "helper" in the church. They went to church at least five times every week when he was a child. "Like Monday was prayer night, Tuesday was band practice, Wednesday was, I dunno, whatever day, Thursday was Bible study, Friday was youth service, Saturday was just a regular service and Sunday was Sunday service. I think there was only one day of the week that I was not doing anything with the church. And 'til this day it is still the same way, my dad and mom are in church every day."

Between the ages of four and five, Dillon was sexually abused by a male family member who was sixteen years his senior, in the family home in Canada. When the family moved to South America, another male family member, thirteen years older, continued the abuse. "It happened from basically the time that I got there until when I left. It was every time I saw him, it happened. It was almost to the point where you just knew it was gonna happen. And honestly just became where, well, I'm not gonna say it was natural because it's not natural. But it just became in a way natural, where you knew that it was just part of your life now." The abuse carried on for four or five years.

Nobody, not even his mother, claimed to know about the abuse, but they should have known — it was happening in their house. In fact, when he finally told his parents about it when he was nineteen, they denied it ever happened. If only someone had taken the time to ask him how things were going at home when he was a child, he could have disclosed the abuse. Instead, it created a seething anger inside him that permeated everything.

Dillon could never figure out why his father never intervened. Perhaps because it was his family members that were committing the abuse, he didn't want to admit to it or make it stop. "I guess I can say that the anger I was building up was a lot towards my dad. Because the father figure, my security blanket, was never there. And things were happening in front of him, like in his house, and he didn't know about it." One of the reasons Dillon never told anyone was that his abusers threatened that if he did, they would kill him.

Not only was Dillon subjected to sexual abuse as a child, but he also suffered physical abuse from his father beginning at an early age. As well as giving him spankings with hand or a belt, his father would make him kneel barelegged on dry rice on the floor for hours while holding a heavy briefcase level with his head. If he rested the briefcase on his head, he would be whipped. "It was pretty crazy . . . it's like I've been tortured." Dillon was ten at the time.

Dillon considers his father's physical violence "punishment," not abuse. And he was the only one who was punished. "I got all the beats in my house. The one that got all the licks was always me. I remember when we just came back from [South America] they caught me skipping school. I was thirteen. I was walking back home; my dad asked me to go to my room." His father was so angry he was shaking. He ordered the boy to go into the room he shared with his brother. "So he told me to go on my knees and face the wall. It was kind of like away from him, the opposite side of where he was. And he said 'just don't look back,' and I was like 'okay.' So he had the belt in his hand and he just started whipping me in the back with the belt. And as I turned around to look at him, it missed my back and went right in my face. I turned back around and said 'What are you doing?' And I could see that he was kind of tearing up but he was still hitting me." Dillon's screams brought his older sister, who was in the living room, running. She shoved herself in-between them and pushed their dad away. Dillon was weeping hysterically, "'cause of the pain, I guess." His sister took him to a doctor who told him to take deep breaths to stop hyperventilating. The doctor asked his sister what had happened, but she didn't tell the whole story and he never reported the abuse. Dillon has never discussed this incident with his sister to this day.

In spite of this treatment, Dillon struggles to put his father in the best possible light, describing him as a role model and a caring father. But he recognizes that his father inflicted real pain. Along with the sexual abuse, his father's punishments "once again took my whole childhood away." Dillon is very close to his father today and doesn't want him portrayed negatively. "He was just doing what he knew to do. I don't blame him for what he did." They have never discussed the violence.

On top of this physical and sexual abuse inflicted by family members, Dillon was terrified by the violent attacks he witnessed in South America. When he was six years old and still living in Canada, the whole family went to visit relatives in South America who were very poor and lived in a slum. One night about 10 p.m., they took a taxi into the slum from another part of the city, but the driver refused to take them directly to their cousin's place, saying "I'll drop you off here, but I'm not gonna go inside the neighbourhood" because of the frequency of muggings and robberies there. It was about a fifteen-minute walk. A truck pulled over to the side of the road in front of them and three men got out. His father pushed Dillon down to the ground, ordering him to stay quiet and not move. One of the men hit his mother and tore her earrings out of her ear lobes. Another grabbed Dillon's sister and choked her while ripping her necklace off. Dillon's father tried to protect them, but the robbers grabbed him by the arms and punched him over and over again. His brother threw rocks at them. His father, who always carried a comb in his pocket, took it out and jabbed it in the face of one of the attackers, and at the same time he kicked the man in his crotch. "They pulled out a knife and they stabbed my dad. And I saw how they actually stabbed him twice, under his belly, you know, and it was pouring blood like crazy. So they ended up running away, and we carried my dad out to the nearest house that had their lights on, and they helped my dad treat that wound." Dillon's father has a very large scar as a result of this vicious attack. He was lucky not to lose his life.

A couple of years later, the family moved to South America where his father had a good job. They lived in an affluent area of the city and had two large Doberman Pinschers for protection as thieves were constantly cruising the neighbourhood looking for targets. In the middle of one night, when Dillon's father was away on a business trip to Canada, a pickup truck pulled up to the house and the people in the truck threw meat laced with poison and pieces of glass to the dogs in the backyard. "My dogs were on the floor and couldn't move anymore." The thieves broke into the house and started to load up their truck with televisions, computers, and other valuables. Dillon woke up to his mother's screams from her upstairs bedroom. "I ran upstairs, and I see that one guy was holding my mom. And then I guess the guy had the kitchen knife, and he is stabbing my mom. And my mom just goes on the floor, and my sister runs upstairs as well. And I guess the guys got scared and started running and my brother runs up and I go to see my mom, and she just fainted." His older sister ran to the family car, where his father always stored a rifle, and fired two shots in the air to alert the neighbours that a robbery was in progress. The thieves took off.

These two incidents left Dillon feeling powerless and afraid. He began to look for danger everywhere, not knowing who would hurt him next. He assumed that he had no control over these events — the sexual abuse, the beatings, the attacks — and in fact blamed himself for not putting a stop to them. The world was a hostile place.

When his family first moved to South America, Dillon was required to repeat grade three because he didn't speak Spanish. He was ashamed and frustrated. He had no friends because nobody spoke English. After two years, he could speak Spanish well and his circle of friends widened. However, he couldn't concentrate in class and started fighting other kids. He was beaten up in three fights; in the fourth he broke his opponent's nose. Because his grades were not good, the school required that parents sign his tests, indicating they were aware of how he was doing. He forged his mother's signature. "I know I did bad things."

When it came time to move back to Canada, his Spanish was excellent but his English was very poor and he was sent to classes for those who spoke English as a second language. He had to repeat grade eight. By this time he was a couple of years older than his fellow students and so he had few friends and didn't talk to anybody. Other students were mean. One said, "Why don't you go back to your country?" One of his few friends demanded, "Why do you let him talk to you like that?" Dillon responded, "Because he always called me a Paki." His friend said, "Do you know what a Paki means? It's an Indian." Dillon knew enough to realize this was a put down. His friend explained the racial slur. Dillon confronted his tormentor: "Why are you calling me that? I'm not even an Indian, I'm Latino." The student pushed Dillon and Dillon pushed back. The fight was on.

Where Dillon lived in South America, few words were exchanged before a fight, unlike in Canada, where there was a fair bit of verbal jousting before boys took the gloves off. In Dillon's experience, fights were all about respect and maintaining honour. "It's just hit, hit, hit, hit, hit, that's it. So I did the same thing here. I mean, I pushed him, he pushed me back, and then I just started punching him. And I threw him on the floor and just starting going nuts on him. I mean one punch after another to his face, and he started bleeding through his nose. I just kept going; I didn't want to and I couldn't stop."

Dillon had been fairly quiet up until that fight, but after it the other kids started to talk to him and look up to him because his tormentor had been one of the biggest bullies in the school. "Everyone started asking me questions, like 'Why don't you join us,' and stuff like that." He developed a core group of close friends who moved with him after grade eight to the same high school and took the same classes. Dillon's violence escalated. "Honestly, all it took was someone to walk up to one of us and say something like 'Hey, you guys are nerds,' and my friend would say 'Are you gonna let him say that to you?' And the next thing you know I'd throw a punch."

Dillon didn't do well in high school. He got very nervous and would "blank out" on tests, so his grades were low. He had ongoing problems with paying attention and staying focused. He had begun skipping class in grade eight and by grade nine was absent more often than not. "I didn't know what skipping class was. I said to my friend, 'Are you allowed to do this?' And he said, 'You can do whatever you want.'" In grade nine, he was absent 143 days out of the 170-day school year. In grade ten, he attended eighteen days in total. "My dad would drop me off at the front door. I'd go inside, put my backpack in my locker, then go out the back door and end up somewhere else." He had to change schools often due to expulsions. He began making money — about $100 a week — dealing weed and smoking lots of it. Some of his friends were dealing and using as well, although they weren't yet a gang.

That changed at the end of grade nine. Dillon founded the gang to create a sense of family with his friends whom he was already working with and for protection from other young thugs. They also wanted to become more organized and increase drug sales. His own biological family was not impressed and he lived on the streets from time to time. He and his five closest friends were the leaders of the Latino gang, recruiting about sixty members in the beginning. Since there was a large Latino population in the city where they lived, it was easy to recruit new members. Within three years, there were 200 members, and they were a thorn in the side of the local police. Their main source of income was trafficking cocaine, ecstasy, crystal methamphetamine, mushrooms, and liquid GHB (gamma hydroxybutyrate). By this time, Dillon was snorting cocaine regularly.

The gang included both young men and women. Dillon and the five other leaders were in control, and everyone else worked under them. They instilled fear in their underlings to maintain "a sense of respect" from them. "We would initiate them, like beat them basically, and once the initiation ended, we would take them to a turf that's not ours, and look for someone that was part of another gang and make them fight." The recruits didn't have to win. "I mean, as long as they put their heart out to represent the gang, then it was good enough. But if they would chicken away and say 'No, I can't do this,' then we would beat them again and say never come back."

The worst beating Dillon ever suffered was while he was still in high school. All his friends in the gang had been expelled, so he was both the only gang member left at the school and the only Latino student there. Most others were black. "And one day I went through the back door of the school, and there was this guy waiting for me. He beat the shit out of me. I took it like a champ, whatever, and then I left, and they told me to get out of the school. The next day I went back, and when I left they were waiting for me with baseball bats. They hit me in the neck, fractured my ribs, my face was bruised and deformed, my legs were beaten so hard I couldn't walk. It was so brutal that I lost consciousness 'cause I got kicked in the face and my nose. I told myself all I needed was to get stabbed or shot, then I'd be good: the cops would have to come to my school to pick me up and drop me off, and escort me for two weeks. [Then] I got hit again." Dillon dropped out of school immediately following this incident.

One of Dillon's friends was the first cousin of a leader in a cell of one of the largest and most violent gangs in America. "Another gang from California had come over to visit and heard about us, and they asked us if we were interested in getting involved with their gang. It was a big gang, and we could just open our own chapter here. So, we said yeah." Four of the five friends who had formed the Latino gang with Dillon moved with him to form the new gang's first Canadian chapter. They were beaten into the gang but, because of the family connection, they got off relatively lightly—although they still suffered serious injuries. They switched to the new gang name. Then, it was their turn to beat in all their underlings. "Like our guys, there were maybe 200 of them. We told them that we were changing over to this gang, and if they wanted to be a part of it we would have to beat them in again. If you don't like it, get lost. So a lot of them said 'Yeah, let's get beaten in.'" Girls were allowed into the new gang and were given a choice of initiation method. They could get beaten in by other female members or get gang-raped in. The gang rapes were "basically an orgy without willing to be participating in it." Dillon never participated in the gang rapes.

The American gang rivalled the Russian and Italian mobs in terms of its organization, international scope, and violence. It took root in California in the 1970s with the migration of South Americans fleeing civil wars in their countries. These refugees did not have access to good jobs — or any jobs for that matter — and lived in poverty. Joining together to protest their unemployment led to camaraderie and unity "but obviously some people took it overboard," Dillon remarked, with an air of banality. After the gang formed in California, many refugees, some of them members, were deported back to their home countries. This helped the gang to spread its influence and size.

Dillon's role as a leader in this gang was somewhat different than the role he had played in his previous gang. "I got this sense of empowerment already, because the name comes with it. I mean you are part of this gang that everybody knows. It's [like] you're walking around with all eyes on you. Right away people on the street make out who you are. And you just gotta be careful. I am walking around with like six eyes on me." Dillon meant that he was a high profile leader and constantly had members of other gangs following him and looking for opportunities to hurt him. He got stabbed many times, shot, and hit with bats by rival gang members. Rather than motivating him to leave, the violence gave him an adrenaline rush that he craved. It made him feel alive. He wasn't bored.

Although he was still involved in trafficking, Dillon now had soldiers to run drugs for him. They were also selling guns and other weapons; robberies and drug rips from rivals (stealing large quantities of drugs from other gangs) were common. Dillon was making $2,500 a week in profit, 30 per cent of which he had to turn over to the California chapter — something that didn't please him. "But I knew that I had to do what I had to do."

One of the benefits of belonging to an international gang was that it afforded protection against rivals, no matter who or where they were. "I mean, you had to be careful about what you're doing, because you don't wanna screw yourself over. 'Cause I mean right now, [the gang] is all over — the United States, Canada, Latin America. So no matter where you go, someone is gonna find you. That's guaranteed." If you contravened the rules of the gang, there was nowhere to hide. The new gang was into hard-core violence, although guns were rare. "It was a lot of baseball bats, chains, two-by-fours, knives. I mean our gang was based on machetes; we would carry machetes everywhere we went. We got into so many fights and brawls, you know we're talking twenty people where some guys come out with baseball bats, and meanwhile we're coming out with machetes. You know, slice or chop someone's leg off, or their tendons up." The fights were "gruesome." One of his guys wrapped a cue ball in his bandana and smashed it into a rival gang member's face, shattering bones. Dillon participated eagerly. "I would blank out. I was in my own little world. I wouldn't even think twice about what I was doing. I sometimes had friends that would say like 'bro, do you remember doing this?' And I would have no idea what I did. It was like I was a different person." Dillon was sometimes scared, but he couldn't show fear to the other gang members. He believes now that the sexual abuse he suffered as a child had an impact on what he was doing. "I think when I was fighting it would be subconsciously there. It's not like I would think of it purposely, you know."

One of Dillon's close friends, a co-founder of the first high school gang, made the decision to form his own gang because he wanted nothing to do with the Californians. He tried to steal as many underlings as he could from Dillon and the other four. Dillon felt betrayed. "So we beat him out, beat the crap out of him, and he became our enemy. And then he divided the gang basically, not a lot, but somewhat, and he walked away with some of our crew, our old crew." This new gang became their biggest rival. Soon after returning from a visit to family back in South America, when he was seventeen or eighteen years old, Dillon went to a party where he ran into this old friend. A brawl started between about fifteen gang members. "All of a sudden someone pulls out the gun and takes a shot at my friend. They shot him in the head and in the arm." Dillon's friend was hospitalized for a couple of months but took up the leadership of his gang when he recovered and continued to be a rival of Dillon's gang.

Dillon had two death wishes placed on him by rival gangs. In the first case, he had sliced the ankle of the brother of the leader of a rival gang with his machete during a fight. The wound was large, and the guy was seriously hurt. He told his brother who had done it and the rival gang leader instructed his members to kill Dillon. A girlfriend of one of Dillon's close friends had relatives in the rival gang and heard about the order. She gave him the heads-up. He left town for a few months and kept a very low profile when he returned.

The second death wish came from the Russian mob. Dillon was partying with ten of his buddies when "this car pulled over and started throwing garbage at us like we were nobodies. So I confronted them." There were four Russians in the car. "So I go 'Hey, what's your problem?' and [the driver] says 'Who do you think you're talking to?' And I said 'I don't give a shit who I'm talking to, what's your problem?' So he opens up the door to step out and I kicked his door for it to close against his leg, and

I basically broke his leg." The other Russians jumped out of the car and the fight was on. Dillon's gang easily won. The brawl was widely reported in the newspapers and other media. A friend had a cousin in the Russian mob and told Dillon that its leader had put a hit out on him. Although nobody ever tried to kill him, Dillon spent many years looking over his shoulder. Even to this day, he says, "I always do [look over my shoulder]. I don't go to certain places."

Dillon believes that he never would have become involved in gangs had a caring adult helped him out when he was a child. His parents never took the time to do this. When he was in his early twenties, friends and other family members told his parents that they needed to talk to him about his childhood troubles. They said, "Hey, you know, maybe instead of judging your son, you should have asked him what's wrong." Teachers were no better. They didn't look at the root of his problems or even ask him if things were okay at home. Dillon described their attitude: "it's like 'why are you skipping school, why are you doing this,' just like pointing fingers."

No one in Dillon's family drank or did drugs. He, however, began at a young age. He was eleven years old when he first got drunk on homemade vodka at a friend's house. He was violently ill that night and the next day. He started smoking marijuana at the start of grade nine and progressed to snorting cocaine by the end of that same year. He says he used on average seven grams of coke each week, although sometimes he would go through this much in a single day. The drug didn't interfere with his ability to lead the gang. "The thing is that the amount I could tolerate was ridiculous. I could consume a gram or two and still be normal. Nobody could ever tell that I was high. And the truth is I probably wasn't high. I was probably just having a little rush." He consumed a lot before fighting because the adrenaline rush was very helpful. In addition to this heavy cocaine use, Dillon drank gallons of alcohol, although he never seemed drunk. "Everyone used to call me a bear, like they would say 'you need a bear tranquilizer to take him down.'" He also smoked weed at the same time he was drinking and snorting cocaine.

Dillon was still involved with the gang when he got married at the age of nineteen. His wife, Susan, had no idea about this. It was not until later that year, when his son was born, that he started to think of what life might be like if he left the gang. "I knew I had to do something, but it was pretty hard at the moment to get out." He didn't know how to leave. He worried that he would be beaten out of the gang so severely that he'd be killed or, at minimum, would have to spend the rest of his life in a wheelchair. It was possible that he could be "honoured" out — basically, the gang might throw him a party and celebrate his exit. When he told his higher-ups in California that he wanted out, he was told to go to a gathering. Dillon was very apprehensive about doing this, but nonetheless he worked up the courage to go. "They tell you that you are invited to go somewhere with all of these guys and you don't know if they're gonna take you to the back of the alley and beat the crap out of you, or if they are gonna take you somewhere nice. You never know. You just gotta go with it." Fortunately for Dillon, he was taken out with honours. The gang held a huge party for him.

But it wasn't easy to leave. The drugs and money kept on pulling him back into gang life. Even when he left, he was still making about $500 weekly selling drugs. To this day he maintains friendships with active gang members. "I mean, to be cut off completely is never going to happen. You're always going to have contact here and there. I'm a little nervous [that I might be pulled back into the life], I'm not gonna lie."

Dillon was not a model husband. He did not treat his wife as well as he could have and he was not very mature. He and Susan had their own apartment and fixed up a room for the baby. "But I still had not grown up. I was not the man that she thought she had married." Some days he just did not feel like going to work so he didn't go. That led to arguments: Susan told him to stop being lazy and start being responsible. One time, they had saved up money to pay their rent. Susan gave Dillon the money and told him to pay their landlord. He ended up blowing it "on coke, and liquor, and girls — stupid stuff." The landlord came to the door and asked for the rent. Susan was confused, and said, "What are you talking about, my husband already paid it." Dillon confessed to blowing the money, but he realized that he had to change his ways. "You know I had to cut back on the drinking, smoking up, drugs, even hanging out with bad friends. Spend more time with family. So I gotta say, my son actually made me a better man."

Dillon went back to school at the age of twenty-four. It wasn't easy. It took him two years to repeat high school but he finally finished grade twelve. When he was twenty-six, he got involved with a youth at risk program, which helped him to cut off his remaining ties with the gang and to complete a business management course. He was also taken under the wing of a supportive police officer who suggested that he re-establish ties with his old high school. The principal invited him to give a talk to students on the dangers of gang life.

Shortly after this, Dillon's second child was born. He needed a steady job. A youth worker helped Dillon write a resume, which was, Dillon confessed, mostly made up: "It didn't really have anything in it. It didn't look pretty. It just said leadership skills. But my worker highlighted all my good things, you know, bilingual, leadership, listening skills, all these things that just looked really good." The worker also coached him on how to be interviewed for a job, especially how to speak. Dillon was used to street language and had no idea how to talk to people who were not in the criminal lifestyle. Not only was his English broken, he used gang-related mannerisms and hand gestures. The worker "told me that I had leadership skills. So he just basically gave me an outline of how I would do things. He found out that they were hiring [at a home renovation store] and he dropped me off for this interview."

Dillon had never worked for anyone in his life. When he got bored in school, he just walked out, so he naturally did the same thing on his first job at a home renovation store. "Like, I didn't tell anyone about it, just left. And then I'd come in the next day, and they'd ask 'what happened to you?' And I would just say 'I had a bad case of diarrhea' or something like that, like always a stupid excuse. And they believed me most of the time. I dunno how I lasted in that job for so long." However, he never got in trouble, learned the products, and came to know the customers. He started to enjoy the job and the feeling that he was doing good work and was respected, especially when other managers asked him for his advice. "They were, like, asking me for my opinion. So I just started to feel respected when people would ask me. I just felt good." He worked hard and was offered a management position. "It felt like I was a gang member again. No joke, like it felt like I had power. The reason that I said it felt like I was in a gang again is because you feel how people hate on you." He meant that other staff members did not like it when he got the supervisory position. "So you feel hate, and it's the same thing in gangs." Dillon's world revolved around power when he was in the gang, and it still revolved around power long after he left. "I mean it felt good. It felt comfortable because I was used to it [the power] from before. The sense of leadership and delegating, I felt a lot more comfortable."

Dillon and Susan split up after thirteen years. The split was amicable and the kids are fine. He attended a wedding recently with his new girlfriend. One of his best friends, who is still a gang leader, was getting married. Dillon was nervous about going because he thought that he might get pulled back into the life. He did get drunk, but his friends respected his decision to leave. "I showed them pictures of my kids. And they were happy for me, you know. They told me that if there was anything I ever needed, they are here for me, and wish me the best."

One of the most important life lessons Dillon learned from his father was to accept criticism. Life can be both ugly and beautiful, his father said and continued "life is like eating a fish. You eat the meat and throw out the bones." Dillon lives his life now according to this motto. "I've learned all of the lessons that my dad taught me and my life taught me, and the bad things I just throw out." Because of the punishments his father inflicted on him, he has never hit his own children. "So with my kids, they never knew what it was to be hit; I've never done that." As far as the sexual abuse goes, he doesn't want to deal with it. "The way I look at it now is like it's done with, and I am never gonna get those years back, so I'd just rather forget about it." Despite his determination not to talk about it, he recognizes how it has harmed him. "I'm weak on the inside. Even when I'm angry, like I'll show it on the outside, but on the inside I'm probably crying." To this day, Dillon does not consider himself to be a violent person. "I mean if you do something stupid I'm gonna react. That's basically what it is."

Dillon has been a motivational speaker at schools, where he teaches kids about the dangers of gang life. He tries to impress on young students the importance of confiding in a trusting adult, especially if they have problems. When he talks with teachers and other professionals, he tells them to ask young people "Is everything okay at home? Is there anything that's bothering you? Is there something that you wanna talk about?" He explains, "I never got that. I think if someone would have asked me if everything was okay at home, or if everything was okay with me, I think I would have poured my beans out. But because I was never asked that one question, I never did."

Dillon now works as a manager at a clothing store, but he would like to be a teacher or a youth worker. As a jazz musician who writes his own songs, he would like to use music in his work with young people. But he doesn't have the money to go to college or university for the necessary professional training. He suffers from low self-esteem, particularly around his family. "My brother is well-educated, my sister is educated. I'm the only one who really isn't educated. My dad is a doctor in theology; my mom is educated as well. They kind of look down on me sometimes, not on purpose, but subconsciously I feel that way." One of his cousins is a child and youth worker. "And it's like, shit, I could've been that. But instead I put my head towards something else that didn't matter. I've got to throw out the bones now."

✳ CHAPTER 7 ✳

MY SHOULDER WAS A BIT SORE FROM THAT ROCKET THING

Gilbert, a compact, muscular Métis man, thirty-four years old, is covered in homemade tattoos. He's a street fighter and, when not in prison, competes in muay thai and cage fights. Cage fighting seems fitting for him because he's been locked up for most of his adult life. He says he feels like a mad dog at times. He's not used to living outside of a pen, and he feels rudderless when not inside prison. It's as if he can't walk straight unless his path is well-defined and narrow, like the halls between cells. "At least in prison I knew when I had to eat, shit, and shower. It was like a fuckin' routine. When I'm out, I feel dazed and stagger around, whether I'm high or not. It's weird."

Gilbert doesn't have many teeth or much facial hair. What little he has on his chin and under his nose he constantly strokes, as if coaxing it to grow. He's been shot at, beaten with a bat, stabbed many times, and had one hand crushed with a hammer and one kneecap shattered with a two-by-four. He has the reputation of being a killer, but if he is, he's never been caught. He is a hustler and has borrowed money from many people, rarely paying them back, so he's not popular. He's been a crack addict since age sixteen.

I first met Gilbert two years ago. I was facilitating a men's group on a reserve in the prairies and he showed up, unannounced, to a group session. He looked like a scared rabbit with a baseball hat pulled halfway down to his nose. His eyes darted around the group, staring through other men. He was either running from something or had heard that there was free food. There were only two empty seats in the room — one to each side of Gilbert. The other men clearly wondered if he really was a murderer and they were afraid to get too close to him. He didn't say one word at the group session, but I started to meet with him on his own in order to get to know him better. He was apprehensive and closed at first, but he quickly opened up.

Starting about age five, Gilbert grew up on the streets of prairie towns; he was constantly on the run from child welfare social workers and the police. He says now that he lived this lifestyle thanks to the influence of his mother who dragged him to bars and left him unsupervised while she drank and traded sex. He often hung around outside and got to know the bouncers and street people. These adults befriended him and taught him how to be a hustler. They gave him drugs to take to their customers, knowing full well that he would never be suspected of carrying dope. The police were constantly on the lookout for him due to his young age, but his street family kept him well-hidden, even from his mother. Eventually he was found and brought back home. When the police discovered that his mother was an addicted prostitute and often left Gilbert hanging out at bars, they called child welfare.

Gilbert had a tough start on life, but says he would not change a thing. His mother drank and did drugs during her pregnancy, which likely resulted in some kind of brain damage. He is illiterate.

Gilbert might as well have stayed on the streets because he never spent much time in his foster homes. "I've been in nine foster homes, for about seven years. One family I was with for two years, another for three years. Then I ran all the time from the next five homes. After I started to run, they sent me out in the middle of the fuckin' bush to a farm. I'd get off the farm, walk through the bush. It took me two days to walk seventy-five miles in the bush. I could do it because my grandfather taught me how to survive in the woods when I was really young. I was not thinking of the animals; I desperately wanted to get back home. I loved my mom. But Welfare came back and took me to another home. I ran. They gave up. They said to my mother, 'Sign here, we're gonna give him back to you 'cause he always ends up here anyway. We can't help him.'"

Gilbert was introduced to muay martial arts by his grandfather at the age of five. He speaks fondly of his first Sensei, a man who spent lots of time with Gilbert as a child. Gilbert credits this man with teaching him all he knows about fighting, including how to make muay thai fighting sticks and nunchuks. He recently died and Gilbert cried when he told me about this loss.

Gilbert was ten years old when he was first exposed to the Warriors, an Aboriginal gang active in the prairies and northern Ontario; one of his uncles was a high-ranking member. Although never a member himself, Gilbert associated with many gangs until such associations no longer had any benefits for him. Chinese, Aboriginal, white, biker, black — it made no difference to him who was in what gang as long as he could make money from dealing their drugs. "I went where the best dope was, where the money was. I jumped from gang to gang, different crews, and I kind of made a lot of people mad. I'm kind of an independent guy. If I thought something was not right, or the drugs were gone, I could go to the next gang. It was back and forth. One crew would be out of dope, and I went to the next to buy dope off of them. I didn't fuckin' care who they were, as long as I could make my money running my crew with their drugs. I'd hit the streets, find my runners, supply them, and bang, bang, bang, sell the dope. I didn't really commit to one gang, joining. I told them 'I'm not here to join. I'll work with you guys; I'll sell your dope."

However, things were not that easy. Higher-ups did not like one of their best distributors hopping from one gang to another whenever it suited him. He didn't care. "I thought everyone understood that — how I worked. They said 'if you are selling our dope, you can't be selling for them. You don't go to other gangs and sell their product.' Basically what I told everybody was that 'I don't give a fuck what you say. If your product is being reloaded in a couple of days, I'll work for someone else until you get your dope ready.' And I never took no shit from anybody. Fuckin' if people didn't like it, it was either we were fighting or I walked away. If they were out of dope, I'd take my profit and go to the next people then. I tell them 'Well, hey, a guy's fuckin' gotta live every fuckin' day. When you guys are done I'll go over there. What am I going to do, starve for the next two days while you guys are getting your product? I'll push this dope and when you reload I'll come back to you.' I'm investing this in them because they have dope."

Gilbert quickly found that gangs didn't like this way of doing business. "People got envious." He was a smart entrepreneur and had his own crew of about eight guys who worked for him for eight years. "We pretty much stuck together. My runners came with me wherever I went. Gangs would beef with me over this because they wanted me to use their own runners. My runners were too scared of me to rip me off, and no one was fast enough to run away from me. They were tough guys."

Gilbert became very proficient at fighting while living on the streets. He fought often, usually over collecting on drug debts and protecting himself from rival dealers and gangs. His crew of hand-picked men are skilled street fighters, and they maintain their fighting skills by practising together at local martial arts clubs.

For a while, Gilbert worked for a black gang. Although he claimed he wasn't a racist, he admitted that he didn't like them. "I can't say I hate those [guys]; I don't mind them but I dislike black people. They are dirty. But how they operated, treated people, fuckin' treated women. They got mad because I was not making a killing for them, but I was doing it for another crew. I just did it for spite." When they were out of drugs and needed to replenish their product, Gilbert jumped to another gang and sold for them for a couple of days. The blacks didn't like this and arranged a "meeting" to discuss matters. Gilbert thought he was being set up, but he wanted to maintain his credibility on the street and went alone. He was confident that his martial arts skills could be put to good use. His crew wanted to come along to protect him, but he said no. "I've never been fearful, but those [guys] ambushed me and I knew it was going to go down. They called this meeting out of town and I went there, and they stabbed me thirty-seven times, all in one day. I went out to meet those [guys] and it was a set up. I knew it was. I still fuckin' went out there. Out of seven black guys trying to kill me, I took four out. I put more fear into them. I hurt them pretty fuckin' bad. They were pissed at me because I'd sell anyone's drugs. They did not like that . . . And I grabbed one guy by his hair and choked him. I crushed his larynx and almost killed him. Blood was spurting everywhere. It was a fearful situation and I was fighting for my life, trying to survive. I was gouging their eyes and poking them. One guy shot me; a single shot .22 [calibre rifle]. I got the gun away from him and beat him with his own .22. I had four guys on the ground. I balled one guy and broke another guy's knee. They never touched me after that." The black gang members took off, cowed by Gilbert's violence.

But Gilbert wasn't done with them. He walked across a couple of fields and found someone to take him to the hospital, where he was stitched up and had a blood transfusion. He was almost dead when he got there due to the amount of blood he lost. "I was down to my last one when that went down." After he got out of the hospital, his family called in reinforcements to deal with the situation. "My cousin heard what happened to me; he knew before I got out of the hospital. So, he sent a bunch of Alberta Warriors, about forty soldiers, down from a couple of places. They found those [guys] at a bar and just about left them for dead. There were four exits at the bar, and all of a sudden all kinds of Indians came through. The manager of the bar was like 'motherfucker, who set me up?' They kicked them unconscious and stabbed those motherfuckers up real bad. They boot-fucked one man outside." After the brawl, Gilbert's family drove him to another part of the province and he lay low for a while. No one was ever charged with anything related to this incident.

Over the years, Gilbert worked closely with one of the most violent biker gangs in North America. He owed them $10,000 after selling a huge shipment of their crack. He had the cash in an envelope and was planning on delivering it to them, but got sidetracked on the way. "I was working for the big guys [leaders of this biker gang]. And I ended up at this place where they [members of a second gang] were, along with this guy they were beefing [fighting] with. I think he lived there because his wife and kids were there. They [the second gang] came in, hogtied him and tortured him in front of his family. Everyone [the family] was screaming. They dragged this guy out to the road by their truck and were going to do him in. He owed them $15,000. I had ten grand and hated it that his wife and kids were seeing all this. I was with the fuckin' gang and was not even thinking of the consequences; I thought it was the right thing to do. I said, 'You let him go and you leave him alone.' I was scared and gave them the envelope. I said 'ten thousand and we're good, okay?' I owed $10,000 to the biker gang and I gave them [the second gang] the ten grand so they would not drag this poor bastard away and kill him."

Gilbert gave away his money to save the man's life and now he had nothing to give the gang he owed the money to. "So I thought, where the fuck am I going to hide? I didn't. I went straight to their [the biker gang] clubhouse where the sergeant-at-arms was. The road captain was there too. I said 'I fucked up. You put dope in my hand and I don't have the $10,000.'" The gang decided to put him through a critical test. "The sergeant-at-arms said 'You're the first person who tells me the truth, ever. You have forty-eight hours to get me $11,000.' '$11,000?' I questioned. 'Yeah, the $1,000 is a dummy tax for fucking up.'" Gilbert asked if the biker gang leaders were going to reload him with another shipment of drugs to sell to get the money, but they told him no.

Gilbert thought he was dead. He had no idea that the biker gang was testing him, planning to give him a patch (a symbol of a gang worn on clothing) if he was able to come up with the money. He contacted his network of clients but no one was prepared to front him. Then, he got a call from an old Romanian friend, Igor, a big-time dealer in Alberta. Gilbert had saved his life the year before. Igor had $100,000 strapped to his waist in a money belt when members from another gang who were trying to rip him off attacked him. Gilbert happened to have his muay thai sticks in his back pocket and scared the attackers off. Igor was lying in a pool of blood, unconscious. Gilbert managed to revive him and drove him to a hospital in Edmonton. "He gave me three ounces of rock, $4,000, and his car for doing that."

Igor heard about Gilbert's problem and met him at a bar.

He said, "I hear you're in lots of trouble. Don't worry, I tell you I help you out. Here's a kilo [kilogram of coke] and I'll give you three ounces to sell at a time. You give me $1,000 on every ounce and keep the rest." According to Gilbert, "That was the best night ever. All fuckin' night the phones were going off. We had two cars on the road. Bam, bam, bam, we were selling like mad." Gilbert made the money just in time and delivered it to the clubhouse. The sergeant-at-arms was surprised and said "We were putting you through a test, Gilbert. We were gonna reload you for free. We just wanted to see what you would do. Do you want a quarter pound to sell? You want to walk away? You can join us." Gilbert said, "I'm done. I'd rather work with my family. We'll still be friends though." The sergeant-at-arms replied, "We'll still ask you to do different things for us. You can still be a soldier if you want." Gilbert said, "I just want to sell your dope, nothin' else."

Gilbert jumped from the gang to work with Igor. "So this Romanian guy came to my place in [the city]. He had two keys [kilograms]. 'I give you one key, Gilbert,' he told me. In two and a half weeks I fuckin' had over $150,000! I had a good crew in [the city]. They were all boxers, kick boxers, Kung Fu. My fucking crack was on fire! The guys [oil and gas workers] were coming in from camps and they had lots of cash. We knew how to find them." But the police were onto Gilbert, and he was well-aware of this. "A couple of cops came to my door but I never kept nothin' on me. I had a safe house down the street at a chick's house. This chick played me big time. She made it look like she was the big fuckin' kingpin. They did a big sting on her and they found nothin'. Then they realized I was the one. It took them three years to catch me because I was always one step ahead of them." Gilbert was charged with trafficking and organized crime, and ended up serving twenty-two months in a correctional centre.

It wasn't long before Gilbert was in trouble with the law again. He was living in a medium-sized city on the prairies and had control over the drug market there. He was running a well-oiled operation, but he had enemies. At a karaoke bar one night, he got into a fight with some guys from a rival crew who wanted to wrestle control of the drug trade away from him. Gilbert had just finished singing and one of the rivals shouted at him "You can't sing, you motherfucking chub." The owner of the club told Gilbert to "Settle down please." Gilbert said, "I'll squash that little fucker outside." When the rival went outside to settle the score, Gilbert met him with a jumping spin kick. "Boom bam I fucked him up bad." A week later, five members of the victim's crew came looking for Gilbert. "Something told me to grab my nunchuks from the bed. At the bar, I punched out their driller and said 'Who's looking for me? I'm right fuckin' here. I'm going out that door right now.' Two guys came out the front door and two more came from the back. I started ripping out my sticks. I'm swinging them around. One guy said to me 'What are you going to do with those toothpicks?' I broke the front piece off his jaw. I finished cleaning them out and they ran. I went home and sawed my nunchuks up and threw them away . . . I played the duck [lay low] for a while. But they [the police] had video of me and I had no choice. They wanted to give me forty-seven months, but I ended up getting eighteen months with no parole. I stayed inside for the whole time and did not get early release."

One of the reasons for this was Gilbert's behaviour behind bars. He was relatively small compared to many other prisoners so he felt he needed to prove himself right away or risk getting shanked [knifed] or beaten up. "The thing is, every jail they [the guards] ask you when you get in 'Are you affiliated with any gang?' I'd say 'I'm IWA.' The guard would ask me what that meant and I said, 'I walk alone, you dumb fuck. Put me in a regular unit with no gangs.' Now all the ranges were organized by gang affiliation. Then the guys [inmates] were thinking they are this and that, and I was small so they wanted to beat on me. They would come in my cell thinking they were going to be my boss; they were going to make me get them canteen [goods] with my money. They said 'Who do you think you are, little fella? Show him like it is you motherfucker.' Fuck that, the first day I pounded four guys in jail. I'm bouncing around, c'mon, let's go. I kicked the fuck out of him in his bag; there was blood dribbling down the drain. I washed my hands and the guards came flying in with their shields. 'See anything?' I said 'nah.' Then people were afraid of me from my first day inside. I could fight. I'm a good-natured guy and I can talk my way into and out of anything. I'm a people person."

The longest Gilbert stayed clear of correctional centres was four or five years. In the late 1990s, he had a pretty stable brick-laying job in Vancouver for a while and was able to keep his crack habit under control. He lived above a tattoo joint and helped out in the parlour after he finished work. He met a "gorgeous" young Greek woman and asked her father, who was in the restaurant business, if he could take her out to a Rolling Stones concert. The father was impressed with his work ethic and allowed the date to go ahead. Gilbert's friend, the tattoo artist, rented a limousine for the night and picked them up. This "impress[ed] the hell" out of his date and her father. "We had front row seats; it was fuckin' great. And after the concert, we got a drive back to my place and she asked me if she could come in! Well, we were together every day for about a year."

Gilbert was a hustler. He had a formula and stuck to it. He bought coke from gangs and made money from his runners and their customers: "I'd pay $1,800 to the gang for twenty-eight grams of powder. That's one ounce. Then I'd cut it back with protein or baking soda to thirty-five grams per ounce, knock it down to street size, which I sold for $100 a gram. So I'd make $1,700 profit for each ounce I'd buy. Then I had to pay my runners, and they got about eight or nine hundred overall for each ounce they sold. So I got $1,000 in my pocket for each ounce. I could dump four ounces on a good night, so I'd make at least $4,000 on a good night. My runners would make about $3,000 to $3,500 for that, so they'd each take home about $500 a night." Gilbert preferred to buy his load as crack, not powder cocaine. He figured that when he had to cook it himself, he lost quite a bit of money, because there was always some coke wasted in the cooking process. If he got a full twenty-eight grams of crack per ounce, his profit margin was bigger. That kind of arithmetic isn't bad for someone whose mother drank and did drugs while pregnant. And he's dyslexic.

Gilbert had his own set of rules and ethics he lived by on the street. "I knew how to make money honestly and unhonestly." He kept his own addiction under control. "I never used when I was working. When I was done for the night, I'd kick back and smoke an ounce." He was always on the lookout for the police and constantly changed his routines in order to minimize the risk of getting arrested. "I had a pretty good system and I ran that city for six and a half years. Sometimes I'd get as much as one kilo to distribute. I'd get paged and I'd be good to go, bam. We had different meeting places for each runner. No one ever came to my place for fuckin' dope. We had pagers, bam, bam, bam." When he needed more money, Gilbert would sell on his own and bypass his runners. He was a good boss as long as his runners did what they were told. "I told them if you start smoking it you're done.' I was the head guy, I'd fuckin' crack their heads if they fucked it up. I said I want this from him da, da, da, da. I owed these guys whatever. 'You come back with this much cash,' I told them. They never dared to fuck me over."

One of the reasons Gilbert was so feared by his own crew and other gangs was his penchant for weapons. After one too many fights, he was given a lifetime ban on owning explosives, guns, and other weapons. "It has to do with dynamite, grenades, AK-47s, and rocket launchers . . . Yeah, fuck, we got a hold of a shipment of explosives and guns. Fuck, we had fun. Throwing grenades and shooting rocket launchers at this abandoned building. It was the middle of the night and we wanted to try them out. Ever shot one? No one got hurt but my shoulder was a bit sore from the rocket thing."

Although he was not supposed to own any weapons, Gilbert kept busy making homemade arms. "Look at this. I sawed in half a piece of three-quarter inch dowel rod, drilled holes at the top centre of each rod, then holes about three inches down, put the rope through and tied knots at the end. Then I got black tape and went all over the fuckin' wood. This is how you fuckin' hurt someone. You grab a hold of the sticks, twirling them around. You can slip the rope around buddy's ankle or wrist, give it a sharp twist, and break buddy's bones. Or, if you want to kill buddy, just twist it around his neck. Give buddy a swinging kick to his knee and then fuckin' surprise him with a backhand strike to his head."

Apart from his homemade weapons, Gilbert's most beloved possessions were two well-worn, dog-eared books: one, a Bible, and the other, a martial arts book given to him by his first Sensei who died three years ago. Gilbert can't read, but the martial arts book has lots of pictures, although the Bible doesn't. Nonetheless, both are well-used. Gilbert was fond of pulling out his Bible and asking whomever he was with to read a couple of pages. He sat attentively, not saying a word, motioning with his hands to keep his companion reading. If you did not believe in God, it was best not to tell Gilbert.

Reflecting on his lifetime of involvement with gangs and crime, Gilbert said, "I turned my life around with martial arts. I learned muay thai when I was five. At age ten I was dealing coke. I never had a really fuckin' childhood. People were showing me how to do this and that and this. I had lots of dealings, lots of different things. Would I want a different life? I kind of wish I wasn't on the street, but I'm not doing bad now. I can work rigs, do slashing [cut roads in the bush], saw, I'm a mason by trade, I can lay brick. I taught myself how to do my own plumbing, build a deck, put in a shower. I'm okay. My family wanted me to join and I walked away from that monkey-ass gang shit. I think I turned out pretty good and can't say I would change much in my life."

Gilbert has recently been released from jail where he was serving time for assaulting the woman he believes is the love of his life, Maureen. He claims that he never really hit her, that she was the primary aggressor. He pled guilty and did the time just to get it over with. Gilbert and Maureen's relationship is a train wreck — they're off the tracks more often than not. When they were apart for five months, Maureen shacked up with four of her previous partners, though not all at once — she just can't live without a man for more than a couple of weeks. Two months after they got back together, they split up yet again. Gilbert claims that this is it, he's never going back to Maureen again.

Both Gilbert and Maureen have been in treatment centres often. They've done well in those programs until they come back home. Maureen has been on probation for stabbing two common-law partners, at different times. She once stabbed Gilbert in his thigh. He pulled the knife out, packed his bag, and limped out of the house, leaving a trail of blood. They made up about two months later. Maureen never did time in a correctional facility for any of her assaults because she was found to be suffering from battered woman's syndrome: she believed that her partners would have killed her if she hadn't fought back.

Maureen is a personable young woman; she is about five feet five inches and 120 pounds. Her hair, light brown with highlights, is perfectly coiffed and her nails are manicured. A smart dresser, she's proud of how she looks. Even when on a drinking binge, she takes care of her appearance — and she's in the habit of bingeing for weeks at a time. She's also had bouts of bulimia. She lives on a northern reserve in a row house. The building has the reputation as a party place. With the exception of the very young children, all the other teens and adults living there are heavy drinkers and crack addicts. The sewage often backs up and floods the basements with a foul stench. Outside is somewhat better. Because the area is not drained adequately, whenever it rains, a muddy lake forms out front — the kind of mud that sticks to boots like clay. Yet, Maureen's small apartment is obsessively tidy. "I'm a clean freak."

Maureen is the youngest of fourteen siblings. Her father has been married to his fourth wife for the past ten years, although Maureen claims divorce is looming. Her mother left her father twenty-five years ago, when Maureen was ten years old.

All of the men in Maureen's life have been abusive. She lost all four of her children to foster care although she tried to be a parent to them once they were old enough to leave their adoptive families and come back home, usually at age seventeen. Her two eldest children have attempted suicide many times. Calvin, her nineteen-year-old son, hung himself two years ago. Maureen pulled him down from a tree branch just in time. He was in a coma for three weeks and sustained permanent damage to his neck, although "his brain is fine." Hillary, age seventeen, intentionally overdosed many times, most recently when using crack with Maureen.

Gilbert and Maureen have two sons — Steven, thirteen and Bobby, fifteen. Two families on the same reserve where Maureen lives adopted them. This drives Gilbert and Maureen crazy. They live so close that Maureen can spit on their houses from her living room. Maureen and Gilbert hate the adoptive parents and claim that they abuse their sons. They constantly tell Steven and Bobby that they are coming back home but this just confuses the boys. Both realize that their parents are severe addicts and are unable to stay clean [free of drugs] for more than a week or two. Maureen is addicted to both crack and alcohol, but alcohol is her preferred escape.

Gilbert recently made a set of nunchuks for Steven. He instructed him to use them only inside his house. "Son, keep them for when you are coming back to live with me and your mom. I'll show you how to fight."

✳ CHAPTER 8 ✳

IF I TOLD YOU I'D HAVE TO KILL YOU

Jeremy is thirty-two, six feet two inches tall, yet weighs only 150 pounds. Skinny as an uncooked spaghetti noodle, his mood is the same: brittle. He looks white but is part Sioux. He has a scraggly goatee and always wears a blue New York Yankees baseball hat. He tries hard to hide his stutter, takes his time talking, and pauses often. He also mixes up words, saying "Vietmanese" instead of "Vietnamese." Although he won't admit it, he is probably dyslexic.

Jeremy had a "perfect" childhood. "I had a great home when I was a kid. My parents were great, they loved me, but I was a little shit. Yeah, they drank, but it was nothing I couldn't handle. They only drank in the afternoons and evenings. We lived on a big farm. Cows, pigs, horses, lots of hay. Fuck, it was okay. My dad never really hit me, just spankings with a belt. When my mom got outta line, he smacked her back into line. Nothing serious." Jeremy fondly remembers feeding the animals and learning how to milk the cows by hand. He told me that there was nothing unusual about his father's behaviour and that it certainly was not violent.

There were more than a few cracks in this perfect family. A family friend molested Jeremy's sister and all his female cousins. When Jeremy was five or six years old, this man and his friend forced him to watch porn with them while they masturbated. Jeremy is not sure if this counts as sexual abuse. Finally, his aunt, who was a "gangster chick," got hold of the man and stomped his head in with her stilettos because she found out about what had happened. Around this time, an adult woman abused Jeremy and forced him to give her oral sex. It happened quite often and the woman threatened to hurt him if he told.

At about age five, his parents decided they couldn't handle him any longer and declared he was out of control. They sent him to live on and off with an uncle, "Crazy Jim." Jim was ex-military. "He got discharged and went squirrelly. He got home from Afghanistan and lived on my gramma's farm in a fucking lean-to. It was in the middle of a field of hay. He refused to come into the house. He took all his gear with him when he left, in a green army duffle bag — his clothes and guns." He practised martial arts on Jeremy and taught him everything he knew about fighting. "He was like a drill sergeant. No one else went near his lean-to but me. He used all these chokeholds and pressure point holds on me. Fuck, it hurt. He'd fucking do it to you, literally show you. I grew up pretty quickly with Uncle Jim. He tortured me for years and my parents thought it was all good. I couldn't tell them what was fucked up because Uncle Jim told me he would kill me. And I believed that crazy motherfucker. He almost killed me. It was torture, that's what it was like. Fuck, that hurt. But I learned at a young age how to take a person down and kill them." He attributes his own proclivity to violence to Crazy Jim. "I was his favourite nephew. We were pretty close besides the fact that he hurt me. It drew us closer. I loved him. He was my best friend growing up. It was tough love."

Despite Jeremy's bond with Crazy Jim, things broke down for an unknown reason and he was shipped off to other family members. Jeremy told me that he made the decision to leave. "When I was twelve, I moved away to live with my aunt and uncle. I kinda fucked that one up because I stole thousands of dollars from them over the years. When I was sixteen, they found out what I was up to and then I kinda got kicked out of the family, you know?" Although he did not initially want to discuss the theft from his aunt and uncle, Jeremy later revealed that they owned a small business and often had cash in the house. Jeremy stole about one hundred dollars per month from them, and his aunt and uncle did not catch on for a couple of years.

By the time he was seventeen years old, he had a serious addiction to alcohol, weed, acid, mushrooms, and cocaine. "I was always looking for my next fix and the money and drugs are easy when you work for a gang." His situation was unique. He looked white but had many family members who were Aboriginal. His older cousins and aunt were involved in three rival Aboriginal gangs, each of which was at war with one or both of the others, and with an Asian gang as well. "'Which one am I going to join?' I asked myself. I had a cousin in [one gang], another in [a second gang], and two of my female cousins had boyfriends in [a third]." Jeremy was able to navigate around these hostilities because of his family relationships and also because he apparently was good friends with the gang leaders. "I sat on the fence . . . it's just friends and family everywhere. Everywhere I rolled, I was related. I was never really [hassled]; no one had to intimidate me. I could go to a party [with one gang] and go across town to [another gang's party]."

When Jeremy was seventeen, he stomped to unconsciousness a man who was suspected of raping his cousin. "I would have killed him, but I just scrambled his brains." He was sentenced to one year in a young offender facility and then an additional three years in a penitentiary. Jeremy was very fond of his cousin and wanted to show her that he could stand up for her.

Jeremy claims to not be racist, but he hates Lebanese people. This is based on his distaste for how he believes they treat women — a bias he picked up at the young offender facility. "They're all fucking dirty scumbags; they are all skinners [rapists]. They'll fucking rape the guy's wife for retaliation, payback. I was never racist or nothing but that's the only race I hated. It started in the young offender centre. The Lebs [a name commonly used in prison by Jeremy's gang] were a big gang. But they never did one-on-one [fights]. They had to get ten guys against one. They lynched me in jail but I got them back — each one individually. I would piss on them and put them out with fire." (Jeremy likely meant that he would light them on fire and then urinate on them.)

Jeremy has no regrets about nearly killing a man. "I'm proud of that. I'll kill to protect women. Doing time for that is an honour. I get a lot of respect in the joint for that. I'd do it again in a second." He is also proud of his sentence. "They said I was on a lifer instalment plan. I was on this range for murderers; the whole unit was for guys who had killed. I was with them! They said I'm max [a maximum security prisoner]. They classify you and score you for this and this and this. I went right from young offender to the max. Then they said, 'You are so young and small we're going to give you medium.' But I got max!" This was a great source of pride for Jeremy. He believed that you had to be more of a man to survive in a maximum-security correctional centre. I think he was also looking for an opportunity to kill someone.

The two prisons where Jeremy would eventually serve six years total — Drumheller and Stony Mountain — both hold about 550 to 600 inmates and they were bursting at the seams when he was there. In both institutions ranges were also organized by gang affiliation. Jeremy committed a number of vicious assaults in prison for various gangs, and he described one incident to me in a nonchalant manner. He was detached but I was on edge. "I was nineteen and stabbed someone who ratted [a gang member] out. He was a snitch and I stabbed him with a hanger. Everyone stood around and were kicking him and just letting him bleed. I kept on stabbing him, poking holes in him. You'd be surprised how much damage a hanger can do when you go in one side and out the other on buddy. There was this other guy who the gang wanted dealt with. I tightly rolled up the newspaper and beat him." In return, Jeremy got protection, weed, oil papers (liquid form of a drug put on blotting paper), and tobacco pouches. "I also got gratitude."

Jeremy was smart on the inside. He always made sure that he befriended the toughest man in the joint by giving him drugs and tobacco. Invariably, the friendship would lead to Jeremy being protected from other inmates. "I was five nine and real skinny. I was just nineteen. I gave this white supremacist [a gang] guy smokes and weed on the bus transporting us from remand to the prison. He said to me, 'I'll take care of you.' And he did." When Jeremy returned to prison for his second stint, the same white supremacist was there; he was the leader of his gang and they controlled the church inside the prison. "If you were white, you had to go. Indians were never allowed to go to church." Jeremy was a chameleon. He acted white when he needed to fit in with the white supremacists and acted Indian with Aboriginal gangsters.

Jeremy earned a reputation in prison for going after rapists. "I beat up skin hounds, I caught notorious skinners. They called me 'Leave it to Beaver.' 'There's a new skinner, get him,' other inmates would say. When I was in Stony Mountain I got this rapist. He was only raping hookers, and then he did a fourteen-year-old at a bus stop, gave her diseases. I choked him out 'til he did the funky chicken — he shit and pissed himself."

Once, Jeremy was sent to segregation for beating an inmate whom he believed was a serial rapist who had been featured on *America's Most Wanted* television show. "I rushed his house [cell]. He wanted to get murdered and knew someone would do it sooner or later. He looked like Stone Cold Steve Austin [an actor and retired professional wrestler]; his eyes were steely blue. I caught him with soap in my sock and beat him. Then I 'Edmonton-*Journal*led' him. You fold the newspaper in a certain way and it's like a club. We got locked down for two months after that. I dunno why I took it upon me; I just did it for shits and giggles. But it's so important to beat these guys. I'm what you call a telephone boxer; I'm good in cells. I just did not like skinners."

Apart from dealing with skinners, Jeremy was involved in more mundane activities on the inside. He got his drugs and tobacco by doing favours for different gangs, especially being on the lookout for guards. "The biggest patch members, from two different gangs, gave me joints for keeping six [watching out for the guards] . . . They were cracking out, getting sick, and I got my drugs."

Jeremy's two sons came from a brief hookup right after Jeremy was first released from prison. They were both apprehended at birth by child welfare and handed over to Jeremy's parents to raise. The mother of the boys took off and has not been heard from since.

Jeremy became a drug runner, transporter, and enforcer for a Vietnamese organized crime group. He also worked for a street gang that provided their muscle. "I was propositioned to get jumped in [inducted — by both Vietnamese and Aboriginal gangs] and was warming up to it. But with the Aboriginal gangs my family were in, it would have been ten gangsters beating me. With the *Vietmanese*, it was only three. I could have gotten my [gang] tattoo. But I didn't. I was already friends with them [the Vietnamese] and I did some dirt for them inside. I didn't want to get told what to do for four years and wait that long to get my full patch. I liked hanging out with these guys."

Jeremy's Vietnamese friends took care of him, unlike his family who were members of Aboriginal gangs. The Vietnamese controlled the prison he was in because they had a stranglehold on the drug network inside. "Who ran the drugs ran the joint," he explains. For any inmate who got out of hand, "It was 'Snap your finger, then I'll snap your neck.'" Jeremy meant that if he got an order from the gang to hurt someone, he would do it immediately. He described how the leaders kept order by escalating their violence. "I had five thousand for bail and they paid it, paid for my bail lawyer, and then there was another five thousand they paid for my appeal bail lawyer. They said, 'Do your time and we'll support you.'" In return, Jeremy had to do a "run" for them. "They gave me something to deliver in return for the bail. They gave me a bag of money and I came back with the bag full of drugs."

Things would have been different if he had stuck with his own family in an Aboriginal gang. "I just seen how some of them [the Vietnamese] operated. They were scared; I was accepted. I'm good with people and treat them good. I was not scared and didn't need to be something. I didn't need to rep [represent] something. I didn't want to be under someone else . . . They let me do what I wanted. The *Vietmanese* took me in like family. They take care of you. My cousin Henry is in an Indian gang. He never got a car, never got dressed up for court in his gang."

"One of the rules in the transport business is 'don't look in the package. Don't touch it or you're dead. We'll cut your finger off.' What did I do? Sometimes I touched it to stay up all night. They knew how I rolled. They knew I touched the product. I'd do a ball [an eight ball of cocaine, that is 3.5 grams, or 1/8 of an ounce] to stay up to work and party." Jeremy claimed that he had approval from gang leaders to violate this basic rule of transporting drugs.

I doubt the accuracy of his claim. Jeremy was the kind of guy who would rip off anyone, even his own kids, to make a buck or get a hit.

On one run, Jeremy looked inside the duffle bag given to him by the gang and discovered thousands of ecstasy pills. He was on his way to the Maritimes. "Ha, ha, ha, I looked. The *Vietmanese* were buying them for one dollar a pill and selling them for thirty dollars each. I stole hundreds and stopped along the way where I could sell. I made $12,000 doing that. Then I had to repackage the pills to make it look like I hadn't tampered with them. I stayed in expensive hotels. I partied, and blew all the money before I got back home." Another time, the bags he was transporting for the gang were very heavy. He opened them and found weapons — AK-47s, Desert Eagle pistols, Glocks, dynamite, and grenades — and thousands of rounds of ammunition. He saw no need to rip any weapons off because he always carried his own handgun and a Glock.

Dawn and Jeremy met just after he split up with his girlfriend, the mother of his two boys. He was twenty-six and Dawn was two years younger. Jeremy was drinking at a strip joint and Dawn was partying with some men in the parking lot. "I was a full-blown addict when I met Dawn. I was already on the pipe [smoking crack] back then. I was instantly drawn to the lifestyle back then when I started to smoke. It was exciting. I said to Dawn, 'Hey girl, want to go party?' We've been together ever since, two peas in two pods." Jeremy was attracted to Dawn because they both liked crack and would do just about anything to get their next fix. They were good company for each other on the street and knew how to hustle for money, food, or a place to stay. They didn't mind this lifestyle as long as they had their drugs.

Whenever someone owed him or the Vietnamese gang money, "I'd go over to buddy who owed me money. I'd tell him I'm here for such and such. 'You have forty-eight hours or I'll

be back with my baseball team. I'll crack you with our bats.'"
Often, he took possessions as collateral. Cars, televisions, stereos,
and drugs — they were all taken then returned once the debt
was paid off. "We'd first snap a finger, so they could still work.
Then, it was their arms and hands. I'd tie them up with a belt
to a chair or a bed. Then crack them with a bat and break their
arms. Whip them with a pistol, use a blowtorch and burn them
a little. Sometimes we'd pour gas around them and I'd light a
cigarette. Never hurt them; it was just threats. Then I'd crush
up their hands with a ball-peen hammer. I had to tape their
mouth shut so we didn't get heated out [attract the attention of
the police]. The message was 'We're gonna come back and kill
you next time.' They shit the bed and there were consequences.
They had to pay the price." Some of the younger Vietnamese
gang members were jealous of his role in the gang. "They were
illegal immigrants, right off the boat. Their families sent them to
Canada. Of course they are not going to become [initiated into
the gang] right away. But I was white and they couldn't understand why I was so well-liked by the head guys. They didn't get
how someone who is white beat them in the ranks. They were
also heat bags [attracted police attention] because they were not
supposed to be in Canada. And they were involved in serious
crime, so the leaders didn't want to invest in them because they
were going to be sent back to Vietnam when they got caught."
Jeremy made much more money and sold a better product on
the street than they did. "I was a better money maker and had
my associations with everyone else. I'd go make the work, not
wait by the phone to go make a deal. They wished they knew all
my connections. The *Vietmanese* always had the best product,
not cut. I could not cut it, break it down. It was good; it sold for
itself. It was number four — heroin. So I got called back; I was
not greedy like they [the new immigrants] were. They thought
we can cut it down by one-half. They were too greedy."

But the Vietnamese leaders "would tell me '*ban la gia din* — you are family.' I could do whatever I wanted with them. They had three restaurants they ran as a front. I could go in with all my friends and eat all we wanted, without paying. They took me in as a family member."

Jeremy maintained close ties with two white supremacist gangs active inside the prisons. However, he denies being racist. "I just always have beefs with black guys and fuckin' Muslims. Once, I had just finished off a drug deal at this restaurant. I was making a run for my buddy. This black guy in an FBI jacket — "Full Blooded Irish" — told me to fuck myself. I chased him and he squirrelled off. I heard 'pow, pow, pow.' My friend shot that black guy in the head. He deserved it but he lived." Jeremy is a complicated guy and I'm not sure how much insight he has into the many contradictions in his life. He is Aboriginal, looks white, and likes the white supremacists, but he works for a Vietnamese gang. He can also ally himself with Aboriginal gangsters if need be.

But the Vietnamese were a cautious bunch. After finishing one run, Jeremy always wanted to get right back on another. The Vietnamese told him no. "I was too hot — attracting police attention. So I went underground on the run [stayed below the radar of both the police and other gang members], but got roasted [apprehended by the police] every time. I had no money then and only ate white bread, butter, and sugar on top. I had to do armed robberies to survive — little ones, about $300 to $400 each."

After four years working with the Vietnamese, when he was twenty-seven, Jeremy attacked a man who beat up his girlfriend's sister. He was sentenced to another three years in prison. Jeremy was lucky to be serving only three years. He had accumulated charges for guns, armed robberies, assaults with weapons, assaults causing bodily harm, and kidnappings. He got convicted on all charges but was able to plead out and serve concurrent time.

"I didn't see my boys for three whole years and my parents fucked them up." He had always had a strained relationship with his parents, but doing prison time sealed their dislike of their son. "My mom and dad wrote me off. I couldn't even make collect calls to them. They didn't even visit once, even when they had my two sons."

Jeremy finished his second prison sentence about a year ago and stopped associating with the Vietnamese gang. "I just told them that I wanted out, and they let me, no problems. 'You are family,' they said to me."

Before they moved to the reserve where Dawn's family lives, Jeremy and Dawn had been living in a rooming house in the lower mainland of British Columbia. They had no money because they were using copious amounts of crystal methamphetamine every day and night. "We had great sex for six hours in a row. The best sex ever. But the meth was so addictive, we couldn't stop." Jeremy put Dawn out on the street to pay for their habit, despite denying to me that he did this. I think he wanted me to believe that Dawn was crazy, and that he was an honourable man. "I never made her; she just did it. She'd only get twenty-five for blowjobs and thirty for straight fucking. We never made much and I don't know why she did it. I didn't approve." Jeremy's two boys, aged nine and seven years, were with them during this time. He had recently got them back from his parents, whom he threatened with violence if they didn't turn them over. They weren't registered at any school. "My boys were great. The drugs [Dawn and Jeremy's drug use] never really affected them [the boys]. We always had food and they had a bed. It was Dawn who was the nut, she was like fucking crazy." Jeremy had to take Dawn to the psychiatric hospital three times over three months. "She got all crazy on the meth and was hearing voices and seeing shit and talking like she swallowed an answering machine. She would say over and over, 'Beep, beep, beep. Don't pick up the phone.'" The boys were apprehended again and returned to Jeremy's parents.

Yet, Jeremy and Dawn were survivors and were comfortable living on the street. Jeremy sold crack — and Dawn. He is not concerned that she has full-blown AIDS and Hepatitis C. Since he has been having sex without a condom with Dawn since he met her, he reasons her tricks can do the same. They have always had unprotected sex. "I don't care if she is sick. I love her and I won't get it." Jeremy seems to believe that he is untouchable and is somehow above serious threats to his life, be it disease, overdosing, or violence. Jeremy was on the street with Dawn when a friend stole his mickey. Jeremy chased the friend down the main street, shouting, "I'm going to kill you, you fucking retard!" The RCMP picked him up and took him to the local psychiatric ward. He was put in restraints and kept in isolation for three nights. When he got out and thumbed his way back to the reserve, cuts were evident on his wrists, likely from a razor. He denies slicing his wrists.

Jeremy and Dawn live on the reserve with Dawn's mother and stepfather. Jeremy snorts Tylenol 3s and morphine, medication prescribed for the stepfather who is terminally ill with cancer. It's hard for Jeremy to contain himself when around her stepfather: he sexually abused Dawn throughout her childhood. He is a skinner (child molester) but Jeremy feels he can't do anything about it. Dawn wants to maintain the peace because her stepfather is dying, and she and Jeremy have no other place to live on the reserve.

My first meeting with Jeremy was in October 2012 at Dawn's parents' house. Dawn had just provided a statement to the local RCMP regarding a sexual assault that happened the night of their wedding, four weeks before. She was the victim. The alleged perpetrator had already been convicted of multiple sexual assaults on the reserve where they live.

When I meet her for the first time, Dawn is thirty years old and is the mother of two girls whom she hasn't seen since they were babies. She is obese, carrying at least 250 pounds on her five feet five inch frame. Her personal hygiene is about as poor as her relationship with Jeremy. She often stares off into space, not making eye contact for minutes at a time. She cries loudly and constantly twirls her shoulder-length hair into knots. Sometimes she shakes so badly, she looks as if she's having a seizure. In addition to having Hepatitis C and AIDS (the latter since she was eighteen), she was recently diagnosed with schizophrenia. She's been prescribed some powerful anti-psychotics to manage her illness — 400 milligrams of Seroquel and six milligrams of Risperidone daily. More often than not, she doesn't get to take it. Jeremy either crushes the pills and snorts it or flushes it down the toilet. He says the medication makes her "grouchy like a bear."

The reserve, about 120 kilometres north of the nearest town, is small and is home to five hundred band members. It consists of about one hundred houses, mostly trailers, for which band members pay about $200 a month in rent. Most are in fair shape and some have been recently renovated. There is also a newly constructed, beautiful band office, paid for in part by the federal government. The band has a large trust fund, mostly from oil and gas companies, which pay the band generously for the right to rape their land. The trust fund used to be much larger, but the wrong people got elected six years ago. They lasted only one term in office. None of them admit to knowing where the money went. The RCMP has been investigating for three years.

It takes ten minutes to walk from one end of the reserve to the other. There are many natural gas wells on the land. Some routinely leak gas, prompting people to evacuate to escape the smell of rotten eggs and the danger from noxious fumes. Some band members have skinny, mangy horses, which are left to run wild around the reserve. Horseshit is everywhere. Stray dogs also run in packs, sometimes after the horses, but more often than not after cars. Kids walk around with bats, hockey sticks, or two-by-fours to protect themselves from the packs.

Dawn and Jeremy got married because he was banned from the reserve last year for selling home-brew alcohol and also for his violent behaviour. The only way for him to be on reserve and not get kicked out was if they married. So they did.

The house is tiny, painted white, and has a small deck off the front door. The doors are missing on all the kitchen cupboards, and none of the drawers have covers. The fridge is empty, save for a half-bottle of cola and a couple of hot dogs, minus the packaging, in the freezer. The sink is overflowing with dirty dishes, frying pans, and a couple of partially eaten hamburger meat patties. In the living room is a large television stand but no television. Dawn sold it for drugs. DVDs are everywhere. There are two small couches and a bed in the corner. The brown linoleum floor is full of holes and dirty.

One of the two bedrooms belongs to Jeremy and Dawn. Dirty clothes are strewn about and food is rotting among the clothes. A purple duvet covers the stained, reeking mattress on the floor. A cat and two dogs run around the house. They are so thin they look anorexic. Dawn's mother says that her daughter and Jeremy are lazy. She wishes they would do chores. Jeremy routinely beats Dawn, who frequently is seen with bruising on her face. He once tried to stab her mother.

Jeremy shakes if he doesn't have a beer as soon as he gets up in the morning. Dawn gets delusional and hears voices if she has no crack for a day. They both say they want to get into treatment. On two occasions I completed all the intake documentation to get them admitted into a treatment centre. On both occasions Jeremy and Dawn went missing right before they were supposed to get on a bus to take them there. They claim that it was not their fault, but instead it was the band who screwed them over by not arranging transportation.

Jeremy maintains that he still wants to deal with his addictions. "I want treatment. I've been sober for six months the longest. I did NA [Narcotics Anonymous] and AA [Alcoholics Anonymous], all the steps. I had five months left on my parole. I fucked it up and instead of going back to prison, I got sent to a treatment centre for five months. I didn't follow some of their suggestions. They said get a dog for a year before you get a girlfriend. I listened to the wrong head."

Conversations between Jeremy and Dawn are punctuated with moments of silence, tears, and screaming obscenities. Talking about his sons, Jeremy turns on her: "Fuck you, you dumb bitch whore. You're fucking nuts, a retard. You're the reason I had to give my boys back to my parents, you dumb shit. I can't believe I got married to a stupid Indian bitch." He raises his fist to her face and shouts, "I'm outta here." When he stomps out the door, Dawn runs after him yelling, "Don't leave me, honey, don't go." The next day it's as if nothing happened. The two of them cuddle and kiss, calling each other the names of cars. "I love you, you Honda," Jeremy coos to Dawn. "No, I love you more, you Jeep," Dawn replies. They embrace again, giving each other long, wet kisses.

Despite the volatile and violent nature of Jeremy and Dawn's relationship, it continues. They both profess their love for each other amidst the abuse, addictions, mental health challenges, and disease. They teeter on the brink of death and destruction, yet neither seems disturbed by it. I think this is in part due to the experiences that shaped both of their lives — they grew up in chaotic and dangerous environments. Their current lifestyle must be familiar and comforting to them.

Jeremy has apparently left the gang, but he hasn't exactly cleaned up his lifestyle. He is severely addicted, often homeless, violent, and regularly involved in crime. He is attracted to prison life because he believes it gives him status and respect. But, each time inside he gets involved with gangs. Largely because of his addictions, Jeremy has no problem doing whatever it takes to get more drugs, even if it means ripping off and harming his own family members. He seems to have no remorse for the victims of his violence. I doubt he will straighten out his life.

CHAPTER 9

FROM CIVIL WAR TO GANGS

Jafar is a tall, skinny young man; he is twenty-nine years old and the father of two young children. He wears his curly hair short and usually has earphones on, listening to L'il Wayne or Young Soulja rap music. He was born in a small village in Southern Sudan and came to Canada with his parents and four siblings thirteen years ago. He is facing deportation because of his involvement in serious crimes in Canada: he headed up one of the most violent gangs in the prairies for a seven-year period between 2001 to 2009. He believes he will be killed if sent back to Sudan because both his mother's and father's families were actively involved in the People's Liberation Army, and most of them were killed by the Central Sudanese government in the Second Sudanese Civil War. "If I go back home, I don't wanna be connected with the military. Some of my mom's family are high-ranking members in the rebel military. The government will kill me." He believes that his parents and older sister were exposed to many atrocities, although they have never talked about this. "My dad became immune to it and never showed any emotion. I know they witnessed horrible things, but they just won't tell me about them."

Born in 1983, Jafar was five years old when he witnessed the murder of many of his cousins, aunts, and uncles. He has vivid memories of these events. "I was born into the war and the war was everywhere: kidnapping and killings happened every day. It was ethnic cleansing. Kids nine years and up were forced to become soldiers. Girls were sexual slaves. I saw dead bodies on the ground — bodies with bullet holes and bodies with heads and arms and legs blown off. One of my dad's family members died in our house. I still remember the noise he was making all through the night before he died. My dad cleaned him up. I remember one time this helicopter got shot down and parts of it landed on me. I ran but I was hit. Now I have a metal plate in my head and I had many surgeries to fix this." Government forces tried to kidnap his parents and siblings. "They tried to kill us, really, and convert us to [become] Muslim. They would come around in trucks and take people in the middle of the night. My parents tried to keep us away from this. At the time I didn't understand why this was going on, but I knew I was not safe. It's all unconscious now, really, and does not cross my mind a lot."

Jafar's parents pursued university degrees in Khartoum between the civil wars from 1973 to 1982. His father was never drafted because Jafar's grandparents hid him from the government and also put all their resources into his schooling. His father completed a law degree and his mother a teaching degree. They both held professional jobs in Sudan during periods of peace.

The family fled from Khartoum to Cairo in 1987 and stayed there for seven years. It was a long and treacherous journey that was over 1,600 kilometres in about four months. "We were refugees and we were moving the whole time. We crossed borders, took trains, boats, and walked for days and days. We finally took a bus to Egypt. I was only four or five and I remember being exhausted the whole time. And we had my baby brother, who was just one year old." The family travelled north from Khartoum to Ombada, and then on to Al Dabbah and Dongola. They skirted the Nubian Desert and then made the long trip to Wadi Halfa. They travelled at night and, during the day, hid from government thugs. After they crossed the border into Egypt, his parents told Jafar that they could now travel in the daytime and didn't have to hide. They took a boat across Lake Nasser, and from there they continued north to Aswan and then, with several stops along the way, they finally reached Cairo.

During their trek from Sudan to Egypt, and while still in Sudan, a male family member anally raped Jafar when he was five years old. He never told anyone about this and believes to this day that his parents have no knowledge of the assault. In Egypt, he was sexually abused again while waiting in line to get food for his family. A man grabbed his buttocks and fondled him. Then, he and his older sister were walking back home from school one afternoon when a group of men grabbed her and yelled, "We're going to kill you and your brother if you don't do as we say." Jafar described how "They took her to some stairs and they all raped her. I watched and couldn't do anything. I thought it was me next."

Jafar never got any help to deal with this trauma. He believes that his sister has never disclosed her rape to anyone either. "As a young person I could not grasp it, but I became more conscious about it and started to think about it as an adult. I remember the pain, and it affects my judgement. I don't know how to deal with it personally. I understand and recognize the effects now on myself and other people around me, but I only did this in the past two or three years. I get really paranoid sometimes at the daycare of my kids and I get suspicious. I'll go onto the Internet and read up on [sexual assault]. I've never told anyone. I now realize that my state of mind, body, and spirit have to be balanced. I started to realize the subconscious part of me. It is a main part of me now, and I accept it."

In Cairo, Jafar's family first stayed in a community centre for refugees. He was enrolled in a Catholic school, which went from kindergarten to grade twelve. He was placed in grade six and struggled because he did not speak the language. Other students bullied him constantly. By the time he turned twelve, he had turned into a fighter. He was failing at school, but was no longer bullied. He had learned to initiate fights instead of waiting to defend himself. "People were so aggressive. To survive I had to fight, sometimes four or five times a day. You have to be a good fighter to protect yourself. And I had my younger brother to protect too. I could not avoid it. They slap you in the neck, say some things, and that's it. They just look at you and you start to fight. You have to do it. It's not like in Canada where you can say 'Hey, you' and that's the end of it. In Cairo, that meant a fight."

Eventually the family moved from the community centre to a house in a low-income area, and thereafter they moved frequently to other houses in Cairo. Life was difficult, and the family struggled to put food on the table. There were violent conflicts between families and also between different ethnic groups. Street fights were common. Jafar's father was not present for much of this time. Jafar didn't know exactly where his father was, but the family did receive letters from him. "I just don't know where he was. He was a lawyer and maybe he was working all the time, but I also know that he had to go back to Sudan to take care of some things." Jafar believes that if his father had been around, he might have been able to deal with the bullying and fighting in a more positive manner.

Jafar bemoans the lack of a father figure. His uncles tried to father him but only made matters worse. "They all like disciplined me. They were not my role models. They gave me whoopings all the time, but it never worked. I would just hate their guts. They were never father figures." The "whoopings" were severe, but it was not only uncles who beat him. His parents beat him also. "I got hit with cables, pieces of wood, really anything around that would hurt me. Back home that's just the way it is. It's not like that in Canada. The worst time was in Egypt and my mom did it. I stole some money to get some food and she whooped me real bad. I was covered in bruises and bumps and it really hurt a lot."

When the father returned from his mysterious absence, the family moved from Cairo to Germany and stayed with a family member for six months. "Frankfurt was a really big city and had long highways. That's about all I know." Jafar did not attend school there. After spending a couple of weeks in England, they landed in Toronto as refugees in 1999. Jafar's parents wanted the family to be in Toronto because they believed it was the best place to give their children a chance of making a good life for themselves. After living in the Regent Park area for one year, however, they moved again to a large city on the prairies. "My parents told me that Regent Park was too violent and that they didn't want me fighting. I remember many immigrant families there and many youth hanging out with gangs." Their new neighbourhood in the prairies had a high proportion of refugee families from Nepal, Ivory Coast, Togo, Cameroon, and Sudan.

Unfortunately, life in the prairies was no better than in Regent Park, and only marginally better than in Cairo, perhaps even in Sudan. The family initially lived in a refugee centre where they had free meals, language training, and recreational programs. It was June, and Jafar was happy there, especially when playing video games. But the centre was located in a high crime area, and many of the youth he befriended were using and dealing drugs. The following October, the family moved again into a social housing project in the north end of the city. "It was okay but it was a rough area." Jafar enrolled again in high school — his third school in Canada in just under one year. "At first, grade nine was awesome." His English-as-a-second-language teacher "really helped me and understood me, supported me in making the transition. She bought me cleats and shin guards so I could play soccer. I was on the grade nine and ten championship teams." English was not overly hard for him to learn because he already had had language courses in Cairo before coming to Canada.

But Jafar could not shake off his anger, nor could he control ongoing bullying and racist slurs hurled his way by other youth. "I was really aggressive and did not want to make friends. I was picked on, then got into a couple of fights with tough kids. Then I picked on them. I did get bullied and I would just fight them. People pissed me off and I didn't know how to cope. I was trying to do good with my grades."

In 2001, Jafar was in grade ten. Halfway through the year, he started to spiral downwards. His parents got on his case because he was constantly in detention at school and being suspended for fighting and skipping class. He dropped out of sports and other school activities. His parents paid little attention because they were rarely home. Not only were they both working in a factory full-time, but his father also drove a taxi and his mom cleaned houses. They sent money back home to Sudan to those family members who were still alive, and it was hard to make ends meet. "They had lots of financial stress with five children. They had to pay off loans to the government [related to immigration], and our water and lights were cut off all the time. They never had money to pay the bills and people were calling about money they owed. They would never see us. We had money for food, shelter, and clothing, but I never had bus money." The father was depressed because he could not get work as a lawyer, and he did not have the time or resources to go back to school to meet Canadian standards to practice law. His degree from Sudan was worthless in Canada. "My dad was not coping with the need for credentials. His career never got back on track. He started drinking and that's when all my troubles started. He was never around and when he was, he didn't act like a dad. Every contact with my parents was over a fight or being kicked out of school. I was always in trouble." child welfare authorities were alerted a couple of times to the family situation — mainly about the lack of supervision and the alcoholic father. People kept coming to his house when his parents were not there and asked questions. Jafar hid his siblings from these people and let his older sister do the talking.

Had his parents been around more often, Jafar might have turned out differently. "I felt rejected at home and knew I was a troublemaker. My parents gave me whoopings even though they were never around to see if I got into trouble or not. I had no purpose in my life, even in my own home. I was on the edge. I started doing marijuana and drinking. I was so angry I would just snap. I was an eighteen-year-old kid and I felt everyone was against me. My parents gave me lectures and told me to sit down. "'I need help,' I told them. They said 'No.' I felt like I had no outlet. I did not have a purpose and I wanted to get away." Jafar dropped out of school and was kicked out of the house. He got a job washing dishes, made enough to get his own apartment, escalated his marijuana use and drinking, and started using ecstasy regularly.

Jafar was hanging out with "bad people" — young black men in their mid-twenties who helped him sneak into clubs and drink with them. Two of them shared a car and an apartment. They told Jafar that if he got his driver's licence, they would lend him their car on the weekends. The only condition was that when they called him, he had to pick them up and take them wherever they wanted to go. He also had to pick up and deliver packages. Jafar soon found out that the packages contained drugs and money. Almost in spite of himself, he was becoming a trusted member of this drug crew. He liked being with other young men who had suffered racism and who had faced the challenges of coming to Canada as refugees. The crew was like a haven from discrimination in the broader society.

Shortly after he became involved with this crew, a violent street gang that did not appreciate the fact that their control over the drug scene was being challenged attacked them. They beat his friends senseless and told them to get out of town. Jafar was somehow able to survive the conflict and was welcomed into the street gang. The gang was composed of young men from Sub-Saharan Africa, most of whom were child soldiers and had witnessed atrocities before coming to Canada.

Before joining, Jafar carefully assessed the gang and "who was who . . . I wasn't really sure if I wanted to be a part of that gang. So, I agreed to distribute drugs and pick up the cash and bring it back to the leaders. I would drive around, they would pay me for my hours, and I decided how to collect my money. Before I joined, I was doing better than their big-time dealers; I was gaining momentum and moving their product faster. I would hold an ounce for them and not rip them off. They knew I could be trusted to make the pick-up and drop-off. I wanted to build trust and I was building up their clientele. I knew which areas of the city and where drug houses were set up."

While Jafar was sizing up this gang, he appealed to them because he didn't have a criminal record, despite his involvement in all kinds of criminal activity. "I was fortunate because of what I was bringing in. Others got recruited, but I joined because of how I was moving their product and making money for them." He was making $700 a night for himself. It took him two weeks washing dishes at a restaurant to make this much money. "I didn't see no point in working two weeks for that. I had my own money; I bought straight from the dealer, forty dollars for a piece [rock of crack] and sold it for $200. I built my own clientele, I had my own product." Jafar was also stealing cars, stereos, and anything else he could get his hands on — and selling them on the street. "I was doing dirt for other people. They'd send me to a house; I'd break in and get whatever I could. They would tell me

FROM CIVIL WAR TO GANGS

'Go to that person and get their money. Go jump this particular individual.' I had nothing to do, and I didn't give a shit." During this time, Jafar became addicted to cocaine, marijuana, and alcohol. He had easy access to drugs and was making enough money to use as much as he wanted. Many times, he would drink until he passed out.

At eighteen years old, Jafar was brought into the gang without being beaten in or doing a "mission" assigned by the leaders. What finally pushed him into joining the gang was the murder of a close friend. Haile was also selling dope for the gang that had a beef with a rival gang over turf. "He was my friend. We were from the same area; we grew up together and shared the same space. Haile knew what it meant to come to Canada as a refugee from a country where war was tearing it apart. There was no protection in the community. This is what I got drafted for [the sense of belonging], what I wanted. I loved this person, and he got killed." The gang was divided over how to avenge his death. So, shortly after he joined, Jafar followed a group of disaffected leaders into a break-away gang. "It wasn't wealth or power. I wanted to be an ambassador, a protector of my 'hood. When Haile got killed, I knew that there was no protection [without the gang]."

Jafar and the other members of this splinter group brazenly wore clothing printed with hate messages threatening the original gang. They also painted graffiti on buildings making death threats against the rival gang that had killed Haile. Their new gang quickly became the largest in the city and spread its tentacles into other areas of the province. "It was crazy, chaos at first. We had dysfunctional alliances on the street, with no connection, and there was a major power struggle. It grew so fast and no one seen it, what it was going to grow into. It took everybody by surprise. There was no established leadership in the beginning, just a few individuals, and no one had overall responsibility. We had four or five guys in charge, whose rank was higher, and then just a really large number of other guys under them." Haile's death produced a crisis and a need for gang members to protect each other. Gang activity in the city exploded.

Right in the middle of this chaos, Jafar was sent to a remand centre on charges for gun offences and drug trafficking. At the time, he was trying to establish some order in the splinter gang and prevent it from imploding. While he was inside, the small group of leaders decided that he would be the best person to be president. They appointed him, and then they visited him at the centre to tell him the news. "They told me, 'You're the boss, you're the one in charge. Everyone answers to you.' I had no choice. I could not reject that. I said, 'Okay, it works for me.' I had to follow their [wish that I take over]. I told them that we had to establish order on the streets. I took care of the gang on the inside, but I said, 'You have to get control on the streets.' I was more the thinker-type person. I was able to unify people on the inside and give orders to unify them on the outside. I stabilized things, basically. Members had to agree to have each other's back. I made the decisions, who is who, and I organized them into rank of secretary, striker, runner. There was lots of transition, and we started to gain momentum on the street."

Jafar was released from the remand centre after four months. His first task was to stop the bickering between high-ranking members. "They were not following orders and I had to stabilize them. Their phone list of customers [for drugs] was not generating a lot of clientele and I had to take care of the paperwork. We had money coming in from drugs, but some people didn't feel like distributing and collecting. I had to sort that out. I had to demonstrate to others how to secure assets and negotiate with people. I had the negotiating skills with rivals." He transformed the gang into more of a military operation, similar to the rebel army in Sudan.

Jafar's gang had three main criminal activities — drug and

gun trafficking, extortion, and prostitution — as did its two rivals. All three gangs were primarily made up of refugee youth from Sub-Saharan Africa. The leaders had grown up together and had been childhood friends. The situation in the city was unique: although each gang had its own leadership structure, the rank-and-file members could float between them. The leaders came to an agreement on this for two reasons: they wanted to work together to maximize profits, and they wanted to put a stop to the murders that were decimating their memberships.

Jafar's gang dealt mainly cocaine, ecstasy, marijuana, and methamphetamine. He sent lower-ranking members to establish and expand the gang's territory by increasing their clientele. He established a line of intermediate-rank members to call the shots and support the lower ranks. Jafar viewed the trafficking of guns as complementary to the drug distribution. "I established connections with [a Mexican gang, a big American biker gang, and local Aboriginal gangs]. I dealt personally with them because it was a more reliable way to do business. We flew under the radar of the police because we worked together and didn't kill each other. People knew people, and we were enemies for sure, but we all needed to buy and sell guns. It was in our own interest to come to terms with them and make an agreement with them. I knew the other high-ranked people in these gangs and said to them, 'Let's make a deal.' My lower-ranked members were told not to start a beef but instead protect the higher-ups. I told them, 'Don't get in our way.'" Although Jafar needed to get along with the leaders of these gangs, he knew that the playing field was not level. "Of course the [other gangs] were much larger, smarter, and more organized. They had guys in charge who were old people, who were experienced and were reliable. They are the most dominant gangs in Canada. My guys were young and not that reliable. I had to tell them to follow my orders or else."

Jafar was not much interested in having women play any key

role in his gang. "They were there, but they didn't have any say, they didn't make no decisions. They were told to not get charged and fly under the police radar. That way we got them to beat up other people, have a car and house in their name, because they were clean. I had a girlfriend and she understood. None of the members had a [driver's] licence and we needed the girls to drive. They had to have a licence. They held money, put it under their name, visited us in prison, and brought us drugs inside. Some loved the lifestyle, the jewellery, and cars. They had to be loyal to the higher-ranking guys."

Jafar was not directly involved in the recruitment of girls into prostitution. But controlling the sex trade was a key money-maker for his gang. "We mainly worked with the owners of clubs and escort agencies. It made lots of money for the gang, and it could increase a girl's status in the gang if she was a pros-titute. Most of them were addicts and it was a good way for us to increase our drug clientele, both if the girls were addicted and their customers were users as well. It helped us establish drug lines in clubs and at escort agencies, but I never paid any atten-tion to that. If a member [lower-ranking male gang member] had ten girls he worked, or a club he extorted money from, it's all just supply and demand — business."

Extortion was the third primary criminal activity of Jafar's gang. Many car dealerships, restaurants, and clubs paid a monthly tax in return for protection from other criminal groups: a guarantee that they would not be hassled by the gang, and an agreement that the gang would direct its members and associ-ates to do business with them. Monthly taxes varied, depending on the size of the business and the amount of work needed to protect and grow it. A typical restaurant would pay $3,000 each month. If the business refused to pay, Jafar ordered members to vandalize the building or beat up customers.

After a year on the streets, Jafar was arrested again and

charged with more weapons offences, trafficking, impersonation, and belonging to a criminal organization. He was sentenced to twenty-three months in jail. Although he entered the facility as president of his gang, he soon found out that he had to deal with many rival gangs inside, including some of the largest gangs in North America. He was no longer the big fish but a guppy among sharks. "There were gangs on different ranges inside. The guards decided to split us up by gang affiliation. There was too much violence and extortion before they did that. I was sent to lock-up many times to separate me from other gang leaders." Jafar's drug abuse continued unabated inside where it was just as easy to get access to drugs as it was on the streets.

While in jail, Jafar received a letter from Immigration Canada summoning him to a hearing where a decision about his deportation back to Sudan would be made. This convinced him that he had to get out of the gang life. His decision was also influenced by a growing feeling of unease about the number of people in his gang being killed by and killing rivals. "We were working out [with weights] and I was with another original member of my gang. People thought I was influential and I wanted to manage the way things worked. People did not care about killing each other — Sudanese, Somalis, Eritreans, everyone from other parts of Africa. [He said to his gang,] 'I decided you guys need to calm down. I'm telling you right now that I don't want to be part of it no more.' I thought to myself I want to deal with my own problems, the deportation order." Jafar asked to be moved to solitary confinement so he could be separated from members of his own and rival gangs. Other members of his gang, who also had had enough, soon joined him. "They said to me, 'We heard you don't want to be part of it. You're facing deportation. That's okay with us.'"

At age twenty-five, after seven years leading one of the most feared gangs in the prairies, Jafar got out. Due to his high rank, his fellow leaders did not oppose his exit, but he was soon to find out that it was a different story with his soldiers and runners. The old gang had changed. "It was fast; it was different. Everyone had guns, vehicles, and the leadership was once again crazy. There were a lot of tensions, literally going after each other, shootouts, machetes, drive-bys. There [had been] at least twelve murders since I joined. They were killing each other, back and forth, back and forth. I lost so many friends, guys I grew up with. It was chaos and I was glad to walk away." Jafar got a lawyer through Legal Aid and appealed his deportation order on the grounds that he was a permanent resident and had served jail, not prison time. His case is still before the court.

The year 2008 was full of changes for Jafar. His girlfriend, another addict, was pregnant and gave birth to a boy that July. In September, he returned to high school (adult education) and began working in a restaurant to support his girlfriend and son. He was still addicted to alcohol and drugs. "It was very difficult, and at the beginning I came to class high and never passed anything. I was so addicted to marijuana and alcohol; it was my main drawback. But my teachers were good and said, 'Come back, come back, don't give up.' I quit weed first and didn't know alcohol was such a problem, but it got to the point where I hated drinking but still drank. I thought I was going to do it on my own, but found myself walking to the liquor store. 'This is not going to be good,' I would say to myself. It was bad. I'd drink two bottles of cognac and about five or six beers on top of that every day." Jafar participated in an outpatient program and attended Alcoholics Anonymous group meetings. It took him four years to get his high school diploma and to get sober and clean. He still goes to AA meetings with his sponsor, who is very supportive. In 2011, his girlfriend gave birth to a second child, a daughter.

For the first two years he was out of the gang, the police questioned Jafar often about crimes they alleged had been committed by his old gang. The lower-ranking gang members questioned him too about why he wouldn't come back. "I was establishing myself to be legit, but lots of people did not like me or trust me. They tried to hurt me; they took my licence plates off my car. They threatened me and said, 'We're going to jump you, make you fight.' The cops were harassing me and it was a pretty rough period. Then there was another hit made on this guy from Sierra Leone, and my gang wanted me back in to deal with it." Jafar had a difficult time with this murder because he knew the perpetrator and the victim very well. But, he was able to ignore his old gang and continue trying to improve his life.

Seven years ago, Jafar's father left his mother and went back to Sudan to practise law. Jafar hasn't had any contact with him until recently; his father disowned him when he learned that he was facing deportation. "I have no connection or attachment to my father. I was the black sheep and I was rejected. Me and my dad are not close. He is a big part of my life and I text him and say 'I love you.' But my dad is not going to change. That's the way he is and I can only change how I respond to him. I just feel that it's not worth it, thinking things will get better, because they won't. I'm okay because I have my own son and daughter now. I'm a parent too, and I make the decisions when it comes to my children."

Jafar's relationship with his mother is somewhat better, but by no means perfect. "I have battles with her over parenting and she, she's a grandparent, she should be supportive. But she's not. It was hard for her coming to Canada where you're not allowed to beat your kids." However, his mother is very generous, parenting not only his younger siblings, but also her own younger brothers and another family member. Recently, she has returned to university for her teaching degree so is not always available to take care of younger family members, a job that Jafar is struggling to fill.

Jafar has just finished a social services college program and has been hired as a youth worker at an agency that supports refugees. He got the job right after he completed a 300-hour placement at the same agency. But the deportation matter hangs over his head and will not go away. "My appeal was dismissed. They said I reoffended within the five-year period, which I did not. They said I didn't show any initiative to get into rehab, which is not true. My life is going to be endangered if I get sent back to Sudan, and I won't be able to bring my kids. I'm the primary caregiver. I have to support my brother, who is eighteen, and my mom is in university. I've asked for a pardon for my criminal record. I haven't offended in three years and I've been clean for that time, too." Moreover, Jafar's ex-girlfriend, the mother of his children, is a drug and alcohol abuser and unfit to look after the children. "She is not stable. I've been explaining to her that alcohol is part of her life and she can't be a good mom. My children almost got apprehended at birth because of her addictions. It was not safe for the children and we were always fighting."

Jafar wants to have a better relationship with his children than he has with his own father. He believes that he can help his children avoid a life of gangs and crime if he is a good parent. "I want to be part of their life; I don't want it to be like my relationship with my dad. I can create quality time with them and spend lots of time with them. My son is real sensitive." Jafar's gang filled a void in his life caused by his parents' neglect, gave him a sense of purpose, and offered him protection. "I had no central guidance. I was rejected by everyone. They [gang members] recognized that I was lost but that I was smart and a leader. They showed me that they had my back."

Yet, Jafar recognizes the barriers that his gang involvement has had and will continue to have on his life. "My criminal past will always hold me back. My own family and my community don't have nothin' to do with me. I have disgraced them. You dishonest them and disappoint them [he said to himself]. It took me two years to realize that gang life was a big lie. Dishonesty and disloyalty in critical situations: I depend on somebody and they fuck me over. You live or you die. It's more of a survival thing. When you decide to abandon your family for the ghetto, the back lane, that's a huge commitment. But if you reject that lifestyle [gang life] and go back to your family and your low-risk peers, it's difficult because gangs accept you right away." Jafar is caught between "two worlds" — gang life and family life.

What has helped Jafar most in leaving the gang life is schooling. "Education is my way out. I know how to live a comfortable life — get myself clean and go on the straight path. Everything I ever wanted I have now; I have control over my life now. I have grown into the man I had envisioned and I accept myself. I have control over my life. I am the person I am growing into." He wants to be a youth worker and counsel troubled teens for the rest of his working life. "I help myself in order to help other youth. They see their life as having no chance and they see that if you can do it, they can too. One youth saw my grad picture and said 'If you can do it, I can too.' Every human being has resiliency and has that ability. When you make that decision and want to get out, it is really, really hard to do that. But it's worth it in the end."

✳ CHAPTER 10 ✳

TERMS AND CONDITIONS

Ivan is forty-one and built like a bull moose. His chest is thick as a barrel. He was once told by the Canadian military, who rejected his application to join, that, "You're wider than you are tall, even with your arms above your head. You are a gorilla." He's an intelligent man, smart enough not to have any gang tattoos, despite being a leader in his gang for the better part of fifteen years. He wears a goatee and has a shaved head. Back in his gang days, he was usually seen with sunglasses and had a closely cropped Mohawk. He was massive then, even bigger than now, and along with his crew, he injected copious amounts of steroids into his thighs every day. He has the telltale signs of someone who has used testosterone and human growth hormones for years: severe acne, an enlarged head, a prominent eyebrow ridge, and mood swings.

Ivan's family immigrated to Canada thirty-five years ago, fleeing a civil war that was ravaging their Eastern European country at the time. Before coming to Canada, Ivan, his brother (who is eleven months younger), and biological parents lived with his grandparents. He was very fond of his grandfather, who was a watchmaker and had a jewellery store at the front of their house. "My grandpa passed on his knowledge to me and my cousin. He gave us jobs to do. He'd dump a massive bucket of screws and nails on the table and tell us 'sort this out.'" Both his grandparents died of cancer and liver-related problems. They both drank heavily, as did Ivan's father.

Ivan's parents divorced when he was about six years old. His father was a "deadbeat, lazy, and a loser. He never worked a day in his life." His mother remarried almost immediately, and his stepfather, whom Ivan called "Dad," adopted Ivan and his brother. His adoptive dad was an engineer. The family immigrated to Canada "for a better life." His younger brother was left behind because of immigration problems, but after two years Ivan's dad "took his buds to [my home country] and found my biological dad. They beat him into a hospital state. The police looked for them for a long time. But my dad was more of a man than anything else. He did what he had to do. I followed him around like a lost dog. He brought my younger brother to Canada after that."

Problems soon emerged. "My adoptive dad was an alcoholic and my mom was clinically depressed because he drank and she took eighty-five milligrams of Prozac every day. Then she turned into an alcoholic. And all my extended family back in Europe were alcoholics. I was the prodigal son of a first-generation immigrant family, but the pride was gone in my family. We were taught to work hard and push [ourselves], but my dad had a disability because of severe back surgeries and a couple of strokes so drank heavily to deal with the pain."

Although Ivan eventually graduated from high school, elementary school was rough. "I was bullied lots and came home in tears. My dad said 'punch him right in the fucking nose,' and my mom told me 'you can't do that.' I had to take things into my own hands. The next time those bullies bothered me, I smashed them in the head with a skateboard. Later, in high school, I would get paid twenty bucks to fight bullies. Kids who got bullied paid me and I would fight in the parking lot." Ivan took to boxing and wrestling in high school. "I became known for fighting and said to myself, 'I don't have to let myself be picked on.' I got into the weights and I was a thick kid to begin with. It was a blessing in disguise. Even though I was five feet eleven and 210 pounds, I got a sense of respect, clout, and popularity with the girls." Ivan also was adept at working on cars and teachers paid him to fix their engines during his last year at high school. But he was also beginning to dabble in crime, dealing in drugs on a small scale. "My school life was mediocre and mundane. Night life was more appealing, even though it was false."

When Ivan was fourteen, a year after the birth of his little sister, his mother told him about her mental illness. "I know she had breakdowns some years after she divorced my [biological father]. It was a brutal break-up and our dog died at the same time. She had him cremated and kept him in an urn. Then, after my [dad] quit drinking for a while, he was in AA [Alcoholics Anonymous] and we were in Alateen [support group for teens who have been affected by someone else's drinking]. My mom lost her Al-Anon [support group for friends and relatives of alcoholics] sponsor. She was in bed for days and days."

Ivan was sixteen when his dad's drinking was at its worst. His dad said, "You need to take care of the family." Everything Ivan had learned until then was from his dad. "My dad was connected to the underground. He was a street brawler . . . he had this other side to his professional life. He taught me to hustle and said 'Don't be a rat . . . You don't let people walk on you, don't hit women, and make sure your family is fed.' He told me 'the police are this and they are that, but you can't trust them. Have a sense of honour and your friends need to take care of each other. There are two things you have in this world: time and what you know. If you waste your time, you are poor.'"

Although he personally never saw his parents fight, Ivan heard yelling and screaming at night and experienced his father's brutality directly. "I never seen [his dad hit his mom] and I did not want to believe it. My dad always said, 'You fight for women and back them up.' When dad was drunk, he made threats, saying 'I'll kill you,' this and that. My dad smacked me and slapped me. I had a healthy fear of him. [He said to me] 'In the Eastern Bloc, you do as you are told, not as I do. You're under my roof, this is how it is.' I was afraid of him." Once, when Ivan was eighteen, he was left in charge of his brother and sister while his parents went out. "As soon as my parents left, my brother and I began beating each other. My dad forgot his wallet and came back. He pulled me off my brother and punched me so hard in my chest that I fell down the stairs and went through a stucco wall. He threw my brother against the rails on the stairway. It was beside a second floor window and he was lucky that he didn't smash through . . . My dad said, 'I will kill you both if I see you fighting again. You are family. Do what you have to do to survive.'"

Soon after this, Ivan and his dad bonded through violence. "I remember one time we got into a fight. We drove to this store and there were lots of East Indian kids there. My dad and I kicked the shit out of them in the parking lot. Some were my friends. I got more respect from my dad after that. I became a somebody. My dad said, 'I'm very proud of you; you fight like a man.'"

A year later, Ivan got a call from his mother for help. "'Come get your dad, he's passed out.' I carried him home, took his clothes off and put him to bed. This was very hard because I looked up a lot to my dad. When he passed away, I had a huge burden on me." After his dad's death, "I felt so obligated to be there, to help. I was paying mom's bills [for cancer treatments] and taking care of my girlfriend. I paid my mom's bills through the underground work — fighting and debt collection. My mom knew and got pissed. 'I provide you with the means to get on with your life and look what you do!' she said. I said, 'I've been my own man for years.' She tried to mother me as if I was twelve."

Ivan's dad was still alive when Ivan first got involved in gangs. "He didn't know the extent and thought that I would not get into guns and drugs. He knew there was fighting and debt collection going on. My dad was proud of me. He didn't know what the money was collected for." However, after his death, Ivan resolved to help his family. "I guess I followed in my father's footsteps. He was the one who told me to support my mom and brother and sister. At the time, I did what I thought was right. I got involved with a crew of guys and did enforcement work. It justified my gang involvement."

It was 1992 and Ivan, twenty-one, was living in his own apartment with a girlfriend. "My sister called and there was yelling and screaming [in the background]. I came over with my girlfriend and tried to reason with my mom. She was throwing stuff in the house. We called the police and ambulance. They put her in a straitjacket she was so violent. She was in the hospital for ten days and then got certified [as mentally ill]. That's when she made me her guardian. The things she was saying, the names she was calling me, were awful. Even the police officer started to cry. The officer told me, 'I'm very sorry but I've never heard anything like this.' My mom threatened suicide. She also yelled that she had been sexually abused as a child. She had never told us about that!"

By then, Ivan had "been in the underground" for two years, "nickel and diming weed and coke, enough to make extra cash on the side." He was working as a bouncer at a strip club owned by a biker gang and was an independent drug trafficker with a crew of twenty men. The biker gang liked Ivan and asked him if he was interested in collecting debts for them. They offered him a lot more money than what he was making as an independent dealer. "It was great meeting the bikers. We had good rapport.

I was kicking ass, naming names. I only saw the cool factor, the promise of a good life, the girls, fast cars, and money. When I was downtown, I never sat in a line to wait; I never greased somebody's hand [paid money to a bouncer]. Bypassing people in line was a high. Everyone respected me."

But Ivan didn't like the rigid structure of the biker gang. "The bikers had a system, prospects [persons being seriously considered for membership] were interviewed and were someone's bitch [had to obey their higher-up] for many years. It was basically a training program. I didn't want to do that and I didn't like it. They offered me a position and I turned it down." Instead, he joined a gang that had close ties with the biker gang. He was neither beaten into the gang, nor did he have to do missions. "You did not have to have wet hands [commit a serious crime] to be a member. Someone had to vouch for you, who knew you, and then members voted on you. They all had to vote you in. The biggest concern was 'what can you bring to the table for us?'" There were roughly 300 members in the gang. They wore hoodies, T-shirts, and jackets with their gang name and insignia when out on gang business.

The gang consisted of young men in their late twenties who were committing serious crimes without much coordination or structure. "My gang had a revolving door with different crews; members were in and out and disorganized. You didn't know who's who in the zoo. That's why it got so bloody [because of all the fighting between and within gangs]. I told my gang that an internal business structure was needed." Modelling the hierarchy from the biker gang, Ivan convinced his buddies to establish the positions of road captain, lieutenant, soldiers, collectors, and enforcers. He was the president. Due to his influence, the gang became more organized and disciplined, at least for a while.

In the beginning, the gang was composed primarily of Southeast Asians and Indo-Canadians, most of them from wealthy families. "They had no business being there. Why are these men so well-off? Boredom. They were served life on a silver platter. Seventy per cent of the people in the industry had no reason. They didn't have to do this." Perhaps their culture led them into gang involvement. "Their relationships were arranged, their treatment of women not good. Most are from very noble families. They have a self-entitled life. The first-born sons could do no wrong. Their moms are cleaning ladies and dishwashers, but their dads have engineering degrees." Ivan quickly "washed out" this ethnic mix by recruiting white guys into his crew. Within five years, the gang was about two-thirds white and one-third Indo-Canadian.

Ivan's specialty was negotiating "terms and conditions" with South American cartels in Peru and Mexico to import cocaine and guns. He also arranged deals with US soldiers who were trafficking in surplus weapons. He typically bought 100 units of pure cocaine from the Peruvian cartel, paying $2,000 per kilo. He would sell it to transfer persons (TPs, or distributors) in Canada for $37,500 to $40,000. "The profit margin was astronomical. I'd identify the TPs and guarantee their shipment. He wants three kilos, for example. Those were the terms. I'd arrange for the shipment to be flown from Peru to the loading bay at [the airport]. One crew was responsible to take it off the flight and deliver it to another crew. That crew was responsible to take the shipment to a safe house. We'd do the same for ephedrine, MDMA [ecstasy], opiates, and other chemicals from Asia." Ivan connected suppliers with buyers, arranged transport, and negotiated the price.

The terms and conditions business was very lucrative. "Once I set up the terms, I collected anywhere from 5 per cent to 7.5 per cent. We made a good percentage. If we had to enforce the terms and conditions, we made 50 per cent. So if a shipment was worth four million to buy, we'd make two million off that." The consequences for making a mistake were severe. "Everyone understood. There was no finger pointing if the shit hit the fan. All knew the consequences. We used people with clean records [no convictions]. If your fingers were on the shipment when things screwed up, it was your responsibility to make amends."

At the same time, Ivan established a system of networking between senior members of rival gangs. Soldiers and other junior members "were too hotheaded" to be trusted to communicate appropriately with rival gang members, but, believing that inter-gang violence was bad for business, Ivan negotiated a truce. "We organized this one meeting and booked the board room of a big hotel. There were seventy of us there, including twelve senior biker gang members, six detail guys [members who arranged financial transactions] from our gang, and the bikers had two detail guys. We agreed that each crew would do their own work and members answered to the leader of their crew. The presidents were not to meddle in these affairs."

Yet Ivan saw, inflicted, and was a victim of, violence. Once, he was on an enforcement job for the biker gang. "Buddy broke into their house, where they were doing their cutting, and took 250 pounds of weed. He also stole motorcycles and [personal water-craft]. We were all packing [carrying guns] and wearing vests [bulletproof]. It was a show of force. We found this kid. He was riding on a motorcycle. We pulled up next to him and [one of my friends] opens his door. He grabbed this kid and put him in the truck. When we got back to our place, we tied him to a chair and asked him questions. 'You were seen on the biker gang's camera leaving their house.' Buddy got the beating of his life and can't use his hands to this day. He had to be taught a lesson. I played the duck [lay low]. I justified it in my head that I did the right thing at the time. I felt sorrow, not guilt, deep in my chest. We kind of squared away. You don't need a Bible to see if it's right or wrong."

On another occasion, Ivan's best friend, Tom, was almost

killed by fellow gang members. Ivan was there and witnessed the whole thing. Six men decided to teach Tom a lesson for disrespecting a murdered gang member. "He was like my brother and he always backed me up. They tied his arms and legs together at gunpoint and then smashed him with an axe. There were holes in the floor and ceiling, and blood splattered like a can of water. It sprayed on the walls. I was on the verge of helping Tom. It could have been me. I wish I could have helped him, but I'd be crazy. Six guys with guns and an axe." Tom survived but spent some time in hospital. He was brain damaged.

Shortly before this incident, Ivan had to settle a score with a fellow gang member who screwed up a job. "He botched a load of guns we were trafficking. He brought them by boat to a safe house, [then transferred them to his car and] stopped at a restaurant on the way. He parked in an area visible to the police, and they found 250 units [guns] in his car. We opted to turn on him. We tied him to a chair and duct-taped his hands to a table. Using pliers and vice grips, we pulled the fingernails out of this guy's hand. I had no remorse. He knew the terms and conditions. What's in your hand is your responsibility."

Another time, Ivan was at a club for a joint party with his gang and the biker gang. "The club was owned by senior members of both gangs. We were trafficking together, controlling our territory. It was trust-building and we were patching over. I walked up to the front and some guy was beaking off [complaining] about this and that. He worked his way inside. I had pending charges and I was tense. This guy is looking at me and he got closer. He made a gesture with a knife across his throat. I snapped and jumped at him over a table. I was carrying a bottle and I smashed it on his head. I beat him. The bouncer intervened and threw us both outside. We both broke loose. Another guy pulled up in his car and I pushed buddy against his door. I used the door to smash his head and shoulders. I split him open pretty bad and he was drenched in blood. There were no charges because the witnesses wouldn't say anything."

By this time, Ivan and his crew were into trafficking steroids and growth hormones because of the money. "The profit margin was the most important thing. And we could vouch for them. Buyers look at us, how muscular we are, and say 'I bet I can get even bigger.' We got our GH [growth hormones] from Sweden and Switzerland. It was $60 to $80 a cycle [a rotation of GH followed by a phase of non-use], and we sold it for $600. We'd sell ten cycles a day, mainly to other crews." They also trafficked testosterone, stanozolol, and androsterone. They bought most of the drugs from a US supplier and brought them up to Canada through the Maritimes; the androsterone came from Russia. They had developed a sophisticated distribution network across the country.

But they weren't just selling steroids; they were taking them as well. "We were cranking [taking steroids] pretty good, taking up to one millilitre of testosterone every two days. Normally you take only one-half to three quarters of a millilitre. All of us were big guys; no one was under 240 pounds. We'd be drinking and using stanozolol, mixing them together, tweaking out. The snap [into violence] is so overreactive that I could not have been stopped or stop myself. When cranking and making [human growth] cocktails for strength and muscle, it's inevitable that you're going to snap out. It was just common for ten to twelve guys in my crew to help each other shoot up [inject steroids]." As well as the steroids, Ivan was heavy into smoking weed and ecstasy, but he never touched cocaine. "I always had a dislike for coke. I made money off it and I didn't care what it did to buyers. I just made sure I got paid. My guys in the crew were told 'don't do it.' We caught one guy doing it and gave him a shit-kicking." He never got drunk in his life because of the alcoholism in his family. Nonetheless, "I was always ramped up [on steroids].

I took more and more and then slowly ramped down. At the peak of my consumption, I was very violent. I could justify anything and my emotional state was not reasonable or logical. We were all on edge at the time. We would meet in a restaurant in a reserved area. We'd bring in girls as a calming effect to keep tensions from escalating."

The gang used young women to seal international drug transactions and keep customers "happy" at gambling houses. They supplied eighteen- to twenty-year-old women to "gentlemen's clubs," and low-level crew members ran girls on the street. Ivan was never involved in any of these activities. "Because I was a specialist for the Peru connection, I would always have at least two girls around for a good time. I used girls as barter and they guaranteed the shipment. The cartel wanted to show us that they were serious as well and also had women around."

Ivan certainly appreciated the never-ending parade of beautiful women who were attracted to gang life. "They were attracted to the $100,000 cars. We would spend $5,000 to $6,000 on a dinner and it was effortless to get them to hang out with us. I probably had thirty girlfriends, but they lasted two weeks at a time. We never forced them and they were free to come to dinner, have drinks, go shopping. The Chinese brought their girls in from other countries, but we didn't have to do that." The gang also used young women with no criminal record to carry guns, hide drugs, drive cars, and gather intelligence on rival gang members. Sometimes one of their girls would lead a rival gang member to believe that she wanted to have a relationship with him when, in fact, all she wanted was to manipulate him into divulging information on his gang's activities.

In the early 1990s, Ivan was sentenced to eighteen months for aggravated assault of a police officer; he got another six months in 2007 for convictions related to operating a grow-op. "My two stints were pretty easy and I never got caught at the scene for the really serious shit I was doing. I didn't have a violent background, at least being caught for it. I was careful, meticulous, when running my end of the business." In his opinion, correctional centres did — and do — little to address gang involvement. "Gangs are everywhere and they are networking all through jail and prison. There's a lack of rehab and you come out with a better understanding of business."

After eighteen years in the gang, Ivan got fed up. He was thirty-six when he started thinking about leaving. "It all started to snowball. A nasty, dirty business. There was no loyalty, no nothing. Brotherhood was false. I could only trust two per cent of the guys. Tom almost got killed at the hands of fellow gang members. My family turned a blind eye to it and my girlfriend at the time didn't like it, but she couldn't force me out. I was shocked at how rampant [the violence] was. Life did not mean anything. I sat down with a friend and he said, 'I'm pretty much done with this.' I just let him go. He was like my brother and I brought him into my crew when he was really young. I gave him the same promise as everyone else got: 'It's a noble thing to do in this world.' But it ruined his life."

By the time Ivan decided to leave, the gang had descended again into a state of chaos. What used to be private business had become very public. "It [gang retaliation and discipline] was no longer behind closed doors. Young guys brought it into the limelight with public beatings and shootings. The bikers didn't want this attention. The new generation didn't follow trends and rules and they could not be monitored. They were self-entitled and living large. At an annual meeting, I didn't recognize half the people there. I heard stupid things, paperwork was not in order, and it was bringing unnecessary heat our way. One crew kicked down a grow-op of another rival crew and it caused problems. Senior members from different crews were ratted out and they fell. Wrong words were said and shit scenarios happened."

Although he was ready to go, it was hard to leave the gang. "Lots of guys are into [gang life] to make a career, but I was only in it for the money. I didn't mind the work, and mine was an easier end. Once or twice monthly I had to discipline guys for a deal gone bad. I went to meetings, dinners, and I networked. The rest of the time I set up deals. I didn't hate my job; I had to be there. My main focus was on networking and making working relationships with different crews in different gangs. There was this big crew meeting once, and players from many different gangs were there. I had a good rapport with different gangs after that. But you can't just get out. It took me three years to slowly wash my hands. I was never really out for the first three years — I chose not to be seen with them. It's only been the past year that I have been out fully. I'd train new guys so there are no voids to fill. It should be a seamless exit from the crew. I consulted with them and trained them, but I was no longer in charge. I was an advisor, and then they eventually said 'We don't need you no more.' But I will always have ties due to friendships and I have good friends that are still in it. I won't commit any offences. If they [gang members] come to my work, I don't want to hear it. 'Get the fuck out of my place.' I can't be around it. I can't have my employees know about it."

Ivan has completed a university degree and is an engineer — the same line of work as his dad. He brings to his current professional job the same business acumen he brought to his gang. "Negotiating terms and conditions in the gang and now in my job is basically the same thing. It's about networking, figuring out who takes care of what details, and making money." Although he has been out of his gang for four years now, he makes just as much legal money today as he did when he was a member. Only today he doesn't have to look over his shoulder.

Ivan has a friend, a veteran gangster, who has just turned fifty years old. "He's an old school thug; it's been his life and all he's known. He's a serious cat and a pretty good player. I made an arrangement with his wife, who wanted to know what's going to happen to her, [and] their daughter, if he gets killed or sent to prison. I said 'I'll have to take care of his daughter.' We bonded for the wrong reasons [the drugs and violence], yet I'd do that out of a bond and respect I have for him."

Perhaps Ivan sees in this friend the dad he still misses. "I hope I am wiser, and can be as good a man as [my dad] was. There is a downfall, you see the light, and you come out on top. I'm thankful I don't have kids yet. I don't want a hustling life for a kid. I love my dad but there's a part of him in me that got me involved in the lifestyle."

Ivan wants youth to understand how dangerous and unforgiving that lifestyle is. "I'd tell kids, 'Do you like the sound of a man's fingernails being pulled off? While he's shitting and pissing himself?' I would sell my soul to the devil not to be there. You swallow your humanity to be a savage. You need to understand the kind of animalism in prison — it's a gorilla factory. You make lots of gang contacts when inside. My friend did time in the USA and he came out a fraction of who he was. Young kids need to hear that. Parents are not doing it [preventing them from glamorizing the gangster life]. It's heartbreaking to me. Anyone can make a kid, but not everyone can parent. There's no rainbow at the end of this. The guys who exit are few and far between. [That life is] not real. The patch on the back doesn't mean shit; the tat [tattoo] on your arm doesn't mean shit. It's not a career, and the faster you can get out, the better. My knuckles are thanking me now. I haven't beaten the piss out of a guy for a while."

Ivan believes that he wasted a good part of his life in the gang. "It was a lie, a huge lie." He's getting married next year to a woman whom he describes as having a good job and a big heart.

He wants to take care of her. She's happy that he is no longer involved in the gang. "She's the single largest reason I'm out. I don't want to fail her."

When I asked Ivan to reflect on his life, inside and out of the gang, he remarked: "Enforcing the terms and conditions brought in the cash but it was like a house of cards collapsing. Now, I work on terms and conditions but in the real world."

✳ CONCLUSION ✳

How do some people end up on a pathway to serious and violent offending? Figuring out the "how" is much easier than understanding the "why" of gang involvement. It involves opening up the dark pages of early childhood and adolescence in many cases. Although not all gang members experience a brutalizing degree of violence — physical, sexual, psychological — at home and in their communities as children, far too many do. Whether they have witnessed, heard, or directly experienced severe violence makes little difference. The end result is that without quality intervention at a very young age, these traumatic experiences leave gaping wounds on the soul.

Unfortunately, most of these children come from families that fly under the radar of child welfare, justice organizations, and social agencies. Why? Some don't want to be identified. Many others don't have the capacity to reach out for help. And some present challenges that don't fit into tidy mandates of helping organizations, so they fall through the cracks of a disjointed system of care.

Spending too much time in the child welfare and youth justice systems, particularly when exposed to anti-social peers, can lead to gang involvement and entrenchment in criminal life. I don't make too many friends when I present these findings at conferences and consultations with government. The child welfare and youth justice systems are supposed to rehabilitate young people, right? Many youth do have successful outcomes, but far too many don't. When I ask gang members where and how they became involved, many talk about being exposed to gang life in secure custody facilities, group homes, and foster homes. Some make criminal connections with other youth and go on to form gangs upon their release. Ivan told me that prisons and jails are "gorilla factories." He stated that there should be no surprises when gorillas are placed in zoos with other gorillas.

Some families have experienced intergenerational loss of children to residential schools, foster and group homes, and young offender facilities. Kim, Janie, Gilbert, and Monica all come from families where generation upon generation of children have grown up in care. The traumatization of breaching family bonds effectively strips one of any capacity to parent. And so the cycle continues. Grandparents, parents, children, great-grandchildren all forcibly removed and placed in a system which is just as bad, if not worse, than their own families.

Experiencing multiple losses, particularly deaths from suicide, homicide, and accidents, is traumatizing for young people. The impact of these deaths becomes more complex when parents of these children are lost to addictions and incarceration. When young people have not been taught how to grieve, or given permission to grieve, the losses pile up like a multi-vehicle accident on a highway. Kim lost both her parents to addiction, street life, and incarceration. She then lost her grandmother when she was apprehended and placed in the foster care system. Her bonding to family and healthy adult role models was ruptured time and again, and this continued while she was in care. Jafar witnessed war atrocities and the deaths of family members right before his eyes. This likely left a traumatic footprint on his brain — it was as if he was brain damaged.

Add in other forms of brain damage — from mothers using drugs and alcohol during pregnancies to being severely abused

— learning disabilities, dropping out of school, or belonging to anti-social peer groups, and the end result is what I call a "snowballing" of risk factors. This can put some young people at very high risk for gang involvement.

Along with brain damage, developmental disabilities and mental health disorders are frequently found in members of gangs. My research is a bit out in left field in this area. I am not aware of much other research that identifies fetal alcohol spectrum disorder (FASD) as a precipitating factor for gang involvement. Of course most people with FASD and other developmental impairments never get involved in gangs or crime because they have proactive parents who provide required supports at an early age. But, for the small number of children who are afflicted with these disorders, and who are also exposed to other risks, serious and chronic offending can result. Janie, Jeremy, and Kim are all good examples.

Some of my participants came from what I call "super gang families." These are biological families where many members are gang-involved. Janie was born into such a family. Her mother was a long-time gang member and an addict as well. Gilbert and Jeremy both have many cousins and uncles who are involved in gangs. Further complicating matters is the fact that in many of these families, members belong to different gangs, which are often at war with each other.

Experiences of deep marginalization and oppression can drive young people to seek out places outside of families for a sense of protection, identity, employment, and belonging. Many gang members grow up in environments where economic deprivation is severe. They tell me that there is never enough food to eat, heat and hydro are often disconnected at their homes, there is no running water, and they never have enough clothes to keep them warm in the winter. They don't like going to school because they look poor and dirty. Many talk of being victimized by racial slurs and being excluded because of their skin color. These young people can turn to gangs to find acceptance and a haven from discrimination. Terrence, Kim, and Dillon told me of such experiences.

But, some gang members, like Ivan and Jordan, never experienced poverty. Terrence grew up in an affluent adoptive home but experienced deprivation for the first two years of his life. Although Dillon's family was affluent, they did experience some poverty when he was a child. Dillon also lived on the streets periodically during his teen years.

Some of you might be curious about, or even averse to, giving some of the most hardened gangsters in Canada a voice. Why is this important? I believe that there are many misconceptions and myths surrounding the circumstances of gang members. It is trendy to think of them as "different" and "not like us." Media outlets and the police like to talk about how these individuals come from "good families," and how there are never any flags indicating trouble in their younger years. All of a sudden they turn bad and become gangsters. This upsets me. I have listened to the life stories of hundreds of gang members and can't think of one case where there has not been some kind of serious problem during childhood and adolescence. Some gang members grow up in affluence, and everything appears to be fine at home. A little digging reveals a family where parents are rarely around to supervise the children, or a child with serious learning challenges. Some gang members come from homes where parents have good, professional jobs. Scratch underneath the surface and you might find domestic violence or addictions.

I often get invited into small communities to help develop strategies to prevent youth from joining gangs and to get members out of gangs. Community leaders tell me that they are drowning in gang problems. I'll bring together representatives of all groups in a community having an interest in the health of youngsters and adults. I always ask the same four questions to this group:

- Who are the top 10–20 adults who are creating the most havoc in the community?
- Are you at all surprised that these people have turned into violent gangsters?
- Who are the top 10–20 youngsters who are giving you the most problems?
- What can you do to ensure that these youngsters don't turn into the same group identified in the first question?

No matter where I am, people respond in a similar way to these questions. Almost everyone knows which kids will turn into gangsters. They are the ones who are acting out at a young age, getting kicked out of school in early grades, and they are the ones who are aggressive and violent to family members and animals. When it comes to the last question, the conversation usually stalls. Professionals love to talk about confidentiality, as if it was the almighty God of justice, school, child welfare, and health sectors. And this is where I get frustrated. I tell people that unless we can figure out an ethical way to work together, and unless we can wrap intensive supports around these kids and their families, we will never be able to prevent these kids from becoming serious and violent offenders. We have excellent research in North America and other parts of the world about quality prevention and intervention strategies with high-risk kids and families. We know which kids will turn into violent and serious offenders, and these same kids are involved in serious trouble at a very young age. Yet, we seem unable, or unwilling, to develop individualized plans of care for these kids and their families that will address their complex needs.

Despite the uniqueness of my ten participants, all of them were troubled in childhood. Some of the troubles were better hidden than others, but the red flags were unmistakable. None of them got the help they needed to prevent their descent into anti-social behaviour and serious crime. Parents and professionals tried in many cases, but these efforts proved futile. Leading psychiatrists gave up on Terrence. Jake never experienced serious consequences for his actions that were full of rage. His parents essentially kept the youth justice system at bay. Monica, Kim, Janie, and Gilbert were taken from their families at a young age and placed into a dysfunctional child welfare system that was incapable of providing them with safe and supportive care. Foster parents and social workers gave up on them because they ran often from foster families. Ivan, Jafar, and Jeremy all had alcoholic caregivers and experienced violence from them. Yet, they remained in dysfunctional families until they were old enough to fend for themselves. Jafar also had to cope with language challenges and the trauma from witnessing war atrocities.

My relationship with the participants is probably a bit of a head scratcher for some of you. My informants like to participate in a process where they are in the driver's seat: they have the expertise on what their lives looked like before, during, and after the gang. They get to review the transcripts from their interviews and also get to look at the drafts of their chapters. At the start I agree to allow them to have a free hand in recommending changes to their stories. I, on the other hand, really control very little. I have power in terms of having the resources to write a book, but I can't do that without their active participation. The writing process I follow is likely very different compared to other authors you may be familiar with.

A few examples are illustrative. Some participants want me to tell the whole world about them, without disguising their identities or their gangs. They want to be in the spotlight and they tell me that they don't give a rat's ass about who knows what about their lives. They want the attention. Kim, who I have known for a long time, is not afraid of anyone and would welcome being challenged by someone in her old gang about her story. She wanted her picture in the book along with pictures of friends in her gang. It took me quite some time to convince her that this was not a good idea. "I'm not fuckin' happy with you about this, Mark," she told me the last time we chatted. Monica is another woman who wants her identity revealed in order to prevent youth from getting involved in gang life and to help hardened gangsters leave the gang. She also wants people to know the identity of the foster father who brutalized her for much of her childhood and adolescence. She understands, however, the possible implications of this. She has many grandchildren in foster homes and group homes, some of whom are involved in gangs. She also has daughters who are attempting to exit gang life. She realizes that revealing her identity could pose challenges for family members.

Terrence is another participant who told me that he had no problems with his identity being revealed, although he did not necessarily want his association with a certain organized crime group recognized. Like Kim, I have known Terrence for a long time. I know his family as well. Terrence asked some of his family members to review his chapter and tell him what they thought. As a result of this, I had a couple of conversations with his sister and brother-in-law about changing some passages in the chapter. They had concerns about him being identified due to a high profile incident that took place in a jail and also were concerned about a biker gang coming after Terrence because of how he described them in his chapter.

Two informants disclosed to me that they had ripped off various gangs — drugs, weapons, and cash — and for that reason they did not want their identities revealed. Jeremy had stolen ecstasy pills from a Vietnamese gang. Gilbert is still looking over his shoulder for enemies he made on the street. He put four men in the hospital after they attacked him. He also is in trouble with an African gang, members of which did not take kindly to the fact that he hopped from gang to gang whenever he wanted, always looking to make the largest profit possible from trafficking cocaine. Like Jeremy, he was a hustler and owed money to many people.

Others are very fearful about their gang exit and what might happen to them if the president of their old gang figures out that they have spilled their guts to me. These informants put much thought into these potential consequences before agreeing to be interviewed. Other participants are happy to have most of their lives revealed in the book, but they want any reference to specific organized crime groups taken out.

Jake fears retribution from a motorcycle gang and also does not want any harm to come to his fiancée. He carefully reviewed every word in his chapter and had very specific feedback on altering details of his appearance — tattoos, hair color, weight. He also did not want his parents to suffer any more trouble than he already has put them through. He also requested that I not write anything negative about his parents, whom he stressed did the best job they could raising him.

Dillon led a Canadian cell of one of the largest and most violent gangs in the world. Although his exit process was a positive one, he does not want anything published that could result in someone figuring out which gang he was a part of. Like Gilbert, he too is looking over his shoulder. Two death threats have been put out on him.

Janie is concerned that her ex-husband may still want to have her killed. He is serving a life sentence for a murder that she witnessed, but she did not end up testifying against him at the trial. She also is in the process of getting her children back from Child and Family Services and does not want anything published that could create problems in this area. But, she also wants to have her identity revealed and that of the man who sexually abused her for many years when she was a child. Janie also wants people to understand that her ex-husband is a child molester, knowing that if this got out he would likely be killed in prison.

Jafar has an upcoming deportation hearing and believes that if he is deported, the government will kill him in his home country. The civil war he fled with his family is still ongoing and the government has killed almost all family members who remained behind. On top of that, he says there is no one in Canada who could take care of his two young children, whom he certainly would not bring with him if he were to be deported. For these reasons, he insisted that I go to some length to disguise his gang and his identity.

Finally, Ivan held a senior position in a high profile gang and was responsible for taking care of business with international drug cartels. He does not want any harm to come to his family or fiancée in the event that his identity is revealed. For that reason he took considerable time reviewing his draft chapter before giving it the stamp of approval.

Giving a voice to gangsters allows for these nuanced stories to come to light. It lets us inside a world that few of us know. It shows us that children are not born bad, but instead gang members are created by adults and systems that harm. Gang members commit monstrous offences but are not born monsters. Of course it is important to hold individual gang members accountable for their crimes, but we also need to understand how social environments can act as training grounds and promote violent offending.

The seven participants who have left their gangs certainly have regrets, while the three others do not. Ivan told me "It was a lie, a huge lie . . . You swallow your humanity to be a savage." Jake said, "People ask me if I miss it and I can honestly say that some parts I do, but the pain and misery you inflict on yourself and the world around you just isn't worth it." In contrast, Jeremy, Gilbert, and Terrence said that they are happy with their lives and wouldn't change much. Gilbert sums this up, telling me "I think I turned out pretty good and can't say I would change much in my life."

Whether or not my informants have left their gangs behind, their voices provide rich details on the complexities of their lives. My hope is that in telling their stories, your perspective will be broadened. If we are able to better understand how some people get involved, we will be in a much better position to keep youth out of gangs and help hardened gangsters leave the lifestyle.

✳ ACKNOWLEDGEMENTS ✳

I am indebted to the hundreds of current and ex-gang members who have been patient with me and told me their stories over the past couple of decades. Although your stories are not part of this book, I have written about many of you in other books and articles. You have opened your hearts and taught me so much.

To the seven men and three women who shared their stories in *Gang Life*, I thought I had heard it all until we sat down and you filled my ears with the diversity of your experiences and your hopes for the future. So, thanks to Kim for your infectious laugh and genuine compassion; to Terrence for your energy, perseverance and athleticism; to Monica for your huge heart and voluntarism; to Jake for your intelligence, self-reflection and honesty; to Janie, whose love for your children and drive to give them a better life is inspiring; to Dillon for your keen desire to break the cycle of abandonment and abuse; to Gilbert, who is not only decent and sincere, but who scares me too much to disagree with anything he says or does; to Jeremy, for the way in which you deal with your daily struggles, and get up each day and simply put one foot after the other (by the way, you also frighten me); to Jafar, who has experienced such atrocities and carries on with a brave face; and finally to Ivan, for your professionalism, both in the gang and out. As you periodically remind me, the only difference now is that your "terms and conditions" are legal – business is pretty much the same.

About six months before my last book *Nasty, Brutish and Short: The Lives of Gang Members in Canada* was published by James Lorimer & Company, the acquisitions editor there, Diane Young, approached me to write another book about gangs. My first reaction was "Are you kidding me! No way." Writing that book had left me feeling like I had been run over by a truck, and I was finally getting to know my family again. Then we started talking about how *Nasty* was a tad too academic, how the stories themselves could captivate readers – and I certainly know enough gang members who are, to say the least, colourful.

Thank you to my daughter Kaila, who is working on her master's degree in social work, and whom I started interviewing for *Gang Life* in the spring of 2012, and who transcribed all the audio files. This was no mean feat given that we interviewed each person for about eight hours. Transcription for each interview took about 35 hours and yielded approximately 60 single-spaced pages of narrative. I owe a great deal to Kaila's dedication and determination to writing the stories down.

I made a deal with each of the people who were willing to be part of this book that he or she would have the opportunity to review their draft chapter and make recommendations before finalizing the text. Much to their credit, the folks at Lorimer accept the fact that this is a critical step in the process of publication. And it is critical: imagine that you are a member of the largest multinational gang in the world. You recently slipped out of the gang, with very little fanfare, because you didn't want to be killed for exiting. Then an affiliate hears about *Gang Life* and figures out that it is you who is spilling secrets on the innermost workings of the gang. The affiliate is not amused and puts out a hit on your life. Or, consider the case of a debt collector or a gun trafficker for a large biker gang. Let's say you helped yourself to some of the gang's money, or maybe ripped some guns off and sold them independently, and then disappeared. You, too, could be found and taught never to do that again in the most final way possible.

There are many other people to thank, and I hope I haven't left anyone out. I will begin by acknowledging the contributions of my dear colleagues and friends – police, social workers, youth workers, academics, policy folks and program administrators. Sergeant Rob "Stretch" Lockhart, Manitoba Gang Awareness Coordinator, RCMP, has been a great friend and collaborator over the years, as has Superintendent R. G. (Bob) Mills, Officer in Charge, RCMP F Division, OSB, Regina. There are many others I wish to acknowledge: Patrol Sergeant Cecil Sveinson, Winnipeg Police; Elder Stuart Amyotte, WonSka Cultural School, Prince Albert, SK; Jami Petit, a social worker with the Prince Albert Outreach Program Inc., has provided invaluable assistance and feedback, with the kind support of her boss, Executive Director Peggy Rubin; Natalie and Kirk Finken of Moment-M, a social enterprise based in the National Capital Region, have provided thoughtful advice and support; David Laird, for decades a First Nations Band Administrator, has been a key ally, as has been Brita Laird, a health planner and nurse with many years of experience. Both David and Brita have provided much support with wine, beer, and laundry facilities; John Ferguson, my dear friend, has always provided insightful feedback on my challenging behaviours; Professor John Winterdyke, Department of Justice Studies, Mount Royal University, has provided critical feedback on a chapter I wrote for his book and went out of his way to undertake a thoughtful review of *Nasty, Brutish and Short*; Professor Craig Bennell, Carleton University Department of Psychology, has provided top notch statistical analyses in our evaluations of gang projects; my friends at the Canadian Police College, especially Craig Nyrfa and Len Busch, have provided kind assistance over the years; Constables Joshua Smith, Nancy Sagar, and Denise Perret from the Fort St. John RCMP have likewise been key collaborators in our gang prevention initiatives; Amar Randhawa and Jamie Lipp from the Victim Services and Crime Prevention Division, B.C. Department of Justice, have been great supports and key associates over the years; Giselle Rosario, from the National Crime Prevention Centre, has provided thoughtful advice on gang project evaluations over the years; and my good friends at the Youth Services Bureau, in particular Dan Pare, have given me a solid foundation in my work for almost two decades. I want to thank you for that. I also want to acknowledge my colleagues at Humber Institute of Technology and Applied Arts, who have given invaluable support and advice. They are: Beverley-Jean Daniel, Denise Gardner, Jeanine Webber, Gina Antonacci, Derek Stockley, Doug Thomson, Christine McKenzie, Corina Ivory, Martha Jansenberger, Aqeel Saeid, Mike Gamble, Greg McElligott, Frank Trovato, Katherine Sloss, Dana Costin, Jessica Gosnell, Olga Greszata, and Alyssa Ferns.

I want to acknowledge the contribution of James Lorimer, Cy Strom, and Kendra Martin at James Lorimer & Company. You have put up with my machinations for far too long. Diane Young, who has since left Lorimer, was instrumental in getting this project off the ground. I want to recognize the hard work of Betsy Struthers, Avery Peters, and Jade Colbert, three of the finest editors around. Your dedication and keen eyes salvaged what surely would have been a train wreck. Thank you.

Last, I want to acknowledge the support and patience of my family: my partner in life and colleague, Sharon Dunn, and our three children, Daniel, Kaila, and Leah. You have been my inspiration for many, many years. You have also told me in no uncertain terms that my book writing has to stop. And it will, at least for now.